Saved By The Enemy

The True Story of Fred & Henry Taucher:
Survival in Berlin Amidst Nazi Terrorism

CRAIG A. LEDBETTER

CLASSIC DAY
PUBLISHING

Seattle, Washington
Portland, Oregon
Denver, Colorado
Vancouver, B.C.
Scottsdale, Arizona
Minneapolis, Minnesota

Classic Day Publishing
2925 Fairview Avenue East
Seattle, Washington 98102
877-728-8837
www.classicdaypub.com

Star of David
"Magen David"

This six-pointed star was made of two interlocking trian-gles. Where the triangles overlapped, it was assumed to be extra thick, offering great protection.

The first known use of the hexagram was as a wax seal in ancient Israel around 6 BC and 2 AD, in a synagogue in Capernaum. Many scholars have tried to trace its origin, with little agreement. One popular legend is that King David used it as a magical shield in battle. Charles the IV of Prague allowed the Jews in his lands to display the star as their own flag on special occasions, and it spread to other areas of Eastern Europe. Eventually, in response to the Christians using the cross to represent their faith, the Jews adopted the six-pointed star to represent Judaism as a whole.

During the Nazi holocaust, the star had its saddest moment. The Nazis chose a yellow Star of David to be worn conspicuously on the clothes by all Jews, to allow easy identification of them. Not wearing it could and would end in death. After the war it became a badge of honor, and it is now used as an amulet of good luck and as a symbol of Jewish identity. It also appears on the flag of Israel and on Israeli ambulances.

Acknowledgments

From Fred:

First and foremost, I wish to thank Patricia. She has actively encouraged me to reestablish my connections to the Jewish community, so that I may share a personal account of lasting historical value. Thanks also to my stepson for putting my family's story together; he showed much patience.

I also must acknowledge Governor Albert D. Rosellini, who served as governor of Washington State from 1957–1965 and is a personal friend and mentor.

Finally, I am grateful for the love my brother shared with me through all those tough years and beyond.

From Craig:

Thanks to Fred for sharing his family's story and to my mother for providing me a good education.

Contents

Author's Word

World War II was never really covered in any depth in my high school classes, and the parents and grandparents of me and my friends really didn't talk much about it to us. I was a part of the generation of post-war baby boomers. It seemed like the "Greatest Generation" just wanted to move on to the dreams they now held, having survived such an enormously long and harsh era of wars. Forgetting about it seemed a lot more important than remembering the pains and sacrifices. Few told stories of those hard times to us youngsters.

In my late teens, everyone was horrified that their sons and daughters, brothers and sisters were now being called to fight yet again, now in some Far Eastern countries that no one knew anything about. I saw the war protestors and the peace signs; this was not a popular war, patriotism was calling just a few. I saw our older brothers getting drafted, as I waited to be of age. I anticipated getting the number in the lottery of conscriptions. For me, that number never arrived. I was to live a life without personally taking part in a war; I missed out on a seemingly never-ending string of major conflicts.

In the Vietnam War, American men and women fought hard and bravely, as always. Close to 60,000 of them would die, and many, many more were wounded. Once again, grown men returned far wiser than when they had left, the military proving once again that it can be a great place to gain knowledge that is useful in times of peace.

I still possessed the desire to know more about my parents' generation. I knew that the war games that I had played as a little boy, taking on the Germans and Russians, were flawed. Killing the Nazis, trapping the SS in foxholes…But wait, didn't the Russians help the Allies win the war? Who were really the good and the bad? What about the Jews, why did Hitler want so very much to kill them? How could such a man hold so much evil?

Luckily, a man joined my family who has many of the answers to my questions. His family had been caught up in the holocaust of WWII, as he was a Jew born in Berlin just hours before the start of one of the nastiest, bloodiest campaigns ever launched against mankind. He and his brother would end up as two of just a few Jewish children who survived those ghastly years right under the noses of their enemies.

During the researching of this book, I ended up getting all the knowledge about this era that I had always wanted and possibly more. I had to reconstruct the events as they unfolded in the proper historical timeline. I had never imagined the grand scale of this reign of terror across Europe and N. Africa. Hitler's Nazis committed genocide: close to 6 million Jews, 10 million Slavs, 250,000 Gypsies, 250,000 homosexual men, and more than 100,000 handicapped persons were the victims. Another 4–5 million civilians were killed as a result of the Nazis' brutal tactics of intimidation and reprisals against anyone who opposed Nazism and the criminally insane Hitler. Who didn't Hitler like? Wow, a total of more than 20 million innocent lives were taken, and that does not include all the many millions of civilian and military personnel lives lost by both sides in the ensuing war.

It was a long time ago, but really not so long ago. It was only 77 years ago that Hitler took power and 65 years ago when he finally surrendered in suicide. Definitely not long enough ago, and forever etched in the minds of those who have survived. There are still quite a few persons who are living today that witnessed this terrible period, and they all hope and pray the world will never enter such a dark storm again.

Learn some of the historical facts of this period of time and experience this amazingly true story of two young siblings who survived against such horrific odds.

– Craig A. Ledbetter

Preamble:
Hitler's Rise to Power

*Anti-Semitism rises against Jews as a race/ethnic group,
not against Judaism as a religion.*

Anti-Semitism is officially adopted by the German Conservation Party in 1882.

In Poland, anti-Semitic laws are passed.

WWI, "The War to end all Wars," lasts from 1914 to 1918.

It is a closely held trench war in which air bombers are used for the first time.

The death toll is extremely high among both troops and civilians.

*On November 10, 1918, Germany's Kaiser flees; November 11 is called
Armistice Day, as fighting ends and a formal peace agreement is signed.*

Germany's general staff won't accept that Germany could lose a war.

*Hitler's anti-Semitic outbursts impress his superiors; they praise him as a born
orator who speaks well in front of large groups, holds their attention,
and sways them to his anti-Semitic views.*

Adolf Hitler was born April 20, 1889, in the small Austrian village of Braunau Am Inn, just across the German border. He was born healthy and a Roman Catholic. During his boyhood, Hitler came across his father's book collection and found a book on the Franco-Prussian War of 1870–1871. He became fixated on this book and considered the war a great historical struggle. He viewed soldiering as the most important occupation that there was. German nationalism was on the rise, especially in the Austrian-German border area. Hitler preferred seeing himself as a German rather than as an Austrian.

The spark that ignited WWI was the assassination of an heir to the Austrian Empire by a German Serb. Hitler was inflamed and immediately enlisted in the Bavarian Army, at the age of 25. Hitler served four years, received two Iron Crosses, and was hospitalized on two different occasions. World War I finally ended with the German Army's surrender. While Hitler was recovering from his injuries, Communist-inspired insurgencies were shaking Germany. A few people even incorrectly blamed the Jews for the revolts. Eventually, the Kaiser abdicated and Socialists took over. Chaos ruled the cities, both in Germany and Austria.

Shortly after the war, German war veterans joined together to create the Free Corps, a paramilitary group, to fight the growing presence of communism. They evolved into the Nazi "Brown Shirts," which became the Nazi Party's army.

Hitler believed that Germany was destined for greatness and the only way to achieve it was to entirely ignore the Treaty of Versailles and rid Germany of all Jews. He joined a military intelligence unit that was supposed to keep tabs on the German Workers' Party. Not only did he watch, he organized it into a strong and viable political party and inserted his hatred of Jews as a large part of its platform.

His new political platform, which held many other points, stated that all civil rights of Jews needed to be revoked and all Jews who had immigrated into Germany needed to be deported. Hitler's anti-Semitism was the cornerstone of his fiery speeches. He used the Jews as scapegoats for the current situation of political instability, unemployment, and runaway inflation and for Germany's defeat in WWI. He found an eager audience, changed the party's name to the National Socialist German Workers Party (NAZI PARTY), and adopted the red flag with the swastika for the party's new symbol.

In 1923, Hitler held a rally at a beer hall in Munich and called for a march on Berlin to rid the government of all Communists and Jews. The support that he was looking for from some Bavarian politicians failed to materialize, and the revolt failed miserably. Hitler was arrested and subsequently convicted of treason and sentenced to five years in jail. He would only serve five months, and while in jail he wrote the first of his two books, *Mein Kampf* (My Battle). In this book he went on and on about Communists, Social Democrats and internationalists, but as always, he saved the majority of his tirades for the Jews. He found them responsible for all the problems and evils of the world. Jews were the German Republic's true enemy, according to Hitler.

Supporters of Hitler arriving at the "Beer Hall Putsch."

Now released from jail, he decided to seek political power through the constitution instead of by force. In 1932, he ran for president and received just 30% of the popular vote, while Paul von Hindenburg received 49.6%, just short of the needed 50%. In the subsequent runoff vote, Hindenburg received 53% to Hitler's 36.8%.

After the election, Hitler and his fellow members of the Nazi Party were determined to bring down the republic and establish dictatorial rule in Germany. They did everything they could to create chaos, and things became so bad that martial law was proclaimed in Berlin.

In July 1932, the Reichstag (Parliament) elections were held and produced a major victory for the Nazis, who won 230 out of 608 seats, making them the largest party. Hitler demanded that he be made chancellor, but President Hindenburg would not comply with the demand because the new party, the National Socialists, did not have a majority, and his view of them was that they were intolerant, noisy, and undisciplined.

New elections were held, and this time the Nazis actually lost ground. Attempting to break the deadlock, Hindenburg appointed Kurt von Schleicher as chancellor. After only 57 days in office, he resigned, unable to get a majority. On January 30, 1933, President Hindenburg appointed Hitler chancellor of Germany, even though his party had only 37% of the national votes, a minority of cabinet posts, and few of the seats in the Reichstag. Hitler and the Nazis then set out to consolidate their power into a dominating force.

On Feb 27, 1933, an apparent case of arson occurred, burning down the Reichstag. Many historians blame the fire on the Nazis, but the communists were blamed at the time. The day after the Reichstag burned to the ground, Hindenburg issued a decree stating "For the protection of the People and the State" the constitutional rights to civil liberty were being suspended. Two weeks later Hitler went before the Reichstag and requested a temporary order granting him the power he felt was needed to deal with this crisis. He obtained the necessary votes and immediately suspended the German constitution. On March 23, 1933, Hitler demanded that the "Enabling Act" be passed, making himself dictator of Germany.

Hitler addresses a rally of the SA.

On August 2, 1934, President Hindenburg died, and the title of president was abolished. Using the temporary power granted to him, Hitler used the Enabling Act to assume the new title of Führer and Reich Chancellor. At that point, he had complete and total power over Germany. Every four years, he would return to the Reichstag to renew his temporary emergency power, which was always quickly approved.

The German people quickly accepted this new order, as most non-Jewish Germans were affected very little by the new laws and decrees. As long as you kept a low profile, worked hard, took care of your family, had your children attend public schools, had them join the Hitler Youth organization, and did not get involved in political dissent, you would have no problems.

Hitler then set into motion a systematic elimination of Jewish civil rights—eventually a total of over 300 decrees were aimed at them—that culminated in the death camps and gas chambers of the 1940s. He also started preparations for Germany to go to war once again as he pursued a policy of expansionism and a quest for the demise of all who he considered enemies to the Aryan people, which included so many.

Sunny with a few clouds: 1931–1933

Chapter 1

In 1930, the IOC awards the Olympic Games for 1936 to Berlin, Germany.

*The first World Cup of football (soccer) is held in Uruguay in 1930;
Germany does not field a team.*

Germany's population is estimated at 64.8 million in 1932.

Unemployment in Germany hits 33%, in 1932.

*Jews are suspect as they hold such a disproportionate
number of the high-paying jobs.*

*Berlin is the center of many new social movements. These movements are
reflected in the arts, sexual freedoms, architecture, and theater.*

Many view the Berlin culture movements as hedonistic, degenerate, and amoral.

*Thousand of artists, filmmakers, designers, and other professionals flee Germany;
among them are 20 former Nobel Prize winners.*

Hank and Fred Taucher could easily have been born in America; instead, they were born in Berlin, Germany, right as the Nazis were coming to power. Hank was only a year old when his brother Fred came into the world, just one day before Hitler became dictator of the republic. The boys' parents were Jewish, and the Nazis' influence was already being felt throughout Germany. Social hospitals in the Reich Land were now reluctant to accept Jewish patients. The boys' parents had no choice but to hire a midwife to assist in bringing their second son into the world at the family's small living quarters.

The reason that Hank and Fred could have been born in America is that their father, Julius, was born on January 13, 1891, in

Manhattan, New York. When he was 19 years old, he immigrated to Germany with his parents. He was then drafted into the German Wehrmacht (Army) during WWI. On April 25, 1917, in the midst of a battle, he was shot in the face. He was taken to a field hospital, where his superior determined him unfit for duty and ordered his transfer to a military hospital in Hamburg, Germany. Arriving on the first of May, he had a month of recuperation, after which he was reclassified as fit to serve again. Fortunately, Julius was left with only a moderate upturn of his mouth, on one side of his face, from the bullet that could have killed him.

While he was recuperating, he received the terrible news that his parents had been killed, civilian casualties of the war. Six months went by before he was reassigned, on January 28, to an infantry unit in Breslau, Germany. When Germany surrendered and WWI was over, he received his honorable discharge, effective February 13, 1918.

Physically handsome might not best describe Julius; his appearance was rather bland or average. He was the product of a hard work ethic, short but with a hard, lean body, always willing to lend his strong hands when needed. In late 1930, Julius met a young woman named Therese, and they were married after a brief courtship.

Therese was petite, at five-foot-three, and carried grace and gentility about her. In fact, with her flawless ivory skin, high cheekbones, warm eyes, and chestnut hair, she embodied the appearance of a younger woman. Such flattering suggestions were as nothing compared to her heart's yearning, which was to support her husband and to successfully start a family with him. Therese adored Julius; he could not have been happier, knowing she had found her bliss in life, and he anticipated a wonderful future. Julius had always respected his parents and all they had provided for him. He had a father who showed strong moral ethics, worthy of being emulated. Julius hoped to convey a similar code by which he lived to the people around him, while anticipating having his own children to guide and encourage toward their full potential, hopefully one day soon.

Therese was the parent of a son from a previous marriage, named Klaus Adolf Wachsner. It is not known whether it was from envy or from wanting to spread his wings some, but as Klaus approached his late teens friction developed between him and Julius. Julius, not wanting to be reminded of Therese's previous marriage, did not care much for Klaus.

Julius had been born into a tradition of shopkeepers and soon found a reasonably priced storefront in which to set up his own business, in 1931. Before long, people knew of his tailoring skills and of his reputation as an amiable fellow who provided an honest service, specializing in both men's and women's apparel. Julius was now in his element, with the shop located within blocks of the main shopping thoroughfare at Kurfurstendamm, in the Charlottenburg District of Berlin. The living quarters were at the back of the shop and were much nicer than the family had been accustomed to: two bedrooms, an indoor bathroom, and a kitchen with a gas cooktop.

A typical Berlin street scene in the Jewish quarters before the Nazi influence.

The future appeared bright to the Tauchers, who were content and happy to have a shop with a living area near one of the most desirable avenues in the city. Now they were within two buildings of one of the largest synagogues in Germany. The neighborhood was predominantly Jewish, but not exclusive; segregation was by choice, not by law. Life looked encouraging. Berlin was then the cultural center of Germany, with a population of approximately 1 million and a Jewish presence of 50,000 to 70,000.

On January 3, 1932, Ernst Henri Taucher, later known as Hank, the first child born to Julius and Therese, was born at a Jewish hospital in Berlin. Everything went well at his birth, and Therese left the hospital after a minimal stay. Fred would be born the next year, though without the luxury of a hospital stay: this detail may ultimately have been the key that saved or at least prolonged some of their lives.

Chapter 2

New Nazi laws and policies approved in early 1933 are put into effect.

Jews are now forbidden to own land in the Reich.

Jews cannot be editors of publications.

Jewish musicians who do not register are barred from performing.

The first call to boycott Jewish businesses is issued by the Nazis.

Nationwide burning of books with Jewish authors as well as any other publications deemed detrimental to the Reich takes place.

Derelicts, alcoholics, and the homeless are imprisoned.

A law issued for the protection of Hereditary Health calls for surgical sterilization or euthanization of anyone with inheritable diseases or malformations.

As the Nazis' new pro-Aryan laws were being put into effect, Horst Alfred (Fred H.) Taucher was getting ready to enter the world. His parents, Julius and Therese, could not find a hospital that would allow the birth of a Jewish child in it, so they turned to a licensed midwife Therese had met due to a recommendation from a Mrs. Müller, who owned a laundry shop where Therese worked part-time. Jews still had their state-issued social insurance cards, which were still valid, but the rumors were that the Jews' cards would probably soon be invalidated.

So on January 29, 1933, in the small living area at the back of Julius's shop, with the assistance of a Fräulein Gertrude Nölting, the midwife, Horst Alfred Taucher was born. He would be known as Fred. Although Fred didn't know it, he had the misfortune of being born just one day before Hitler became the chancellor of Germany. It would be a few years before Fred would learn of the enormity of this bit of bad luck.

Gertrude would become a lot more than a midwife to the Tauchers as the years unfolded. Slowly, parts of her life, truly terrifying parts, would be revealed to some of the family. The mystery surrounding her was really beyond comprehension; it was something that was only speculated upon by Therese and Julius, behind closed doors. The boys, being so young, remained clueless about Gertrude's true persuasions, never knowing that so much danger could be found so close.

Both Hank and Fred were, thankfully, born healthy and were lavished with love. As in many cultures, in Judaism male children are viewed as most fortunate and as the means by which the family lineage can continue. It did not matter to Hitler that most Jews in Germany at that time felt themselves to be quite cosmopolitan and considered themselves Germans first and Jews only by religion; some were married to non-Jewish Germans, which, although it was frowned upon by all, was not yet against the law of Germany. Thousands of Jews had fought for the fatherland, with many earning honors and many dying bravely for it in WWI.

The Jewish community had helped propel Germany to the top in many fields of science, physics, medicine, and academics as well as in the arts and numerous other fields. In Hitler's and his fellow Nazis' minds, Jews were the enemies of Germany and of all of the rest of the world and must be destroyed. Hitler called for them to be persecuted and exterminated. This was the first real warning light in the Tauchers' peaceful life that things might be changing. Just how much no one knew. The boys, so young, were clueless.

Just days after becoming chancellor, Hitler ordered that all Jewish-owned stores be boycotted. The boycott began on the morning of April 1, 1933, when Nazi troops were posted at the entrances of shops, offices, and other businesses that Jews owned. Being Saturday, there was little effect, as most Jewish businesses closed for the Sabbath anyway. The boycott lasted only one day. The boycott, in reality, only marked the rapid start of Nazi repression. During Hitler's 12 years of rule, over 300 laws and restrictions would be put in place against the Jewish people and others who lived in the Reich Land, throughout Eastern and Western Europe.

Members of the SA take to the streets of towns across Germany to enforce the boycott of Jewish-owned business.

A week after the failed boycott, "The Law of the Restoration of Civil Service" took effect, prohibiting Jews from holding any civil positions of employment. Quickly, Jews were summarily dismissed. As a result, Jews were prohibited from acting as lawyers and could not serve in state-run hospitals and clinics as doctors. Then, Jews were restricted from attending most schools, to reduce overcrowding in the German public schools. Jewish dentists and their assistants were also prohibited from working in state-run institutions. Then, university professors, notaries, and lecturers were restricted. Soon, all non-Aryans and their families were prohibited from any type of government employment.

Starting in mid-fall, Jews could not attend cultural events and other entertainment activities. Jews were then prohibited from being journalists, and all German newspapers were placed under Nazi control. Jews were not even permitted to sit on park benches that an Aryan was already sitting on. Eventually, a few benches were painted a special color designating their use for Jews only. No one was ever seen using these, for obvious reasons. Parks, sporting events, cultural events, and beaches were all closed to Jews.

It didn't take Hitler long to turn Germany into a police state, the likes of which had never been seen before. Both Germans and Jews quickly found themselves living in one of the most repressive and grossly violent eras ever known to man. Hitler, his Nazis, and his secret police (the Gestapo) had total control and were bent on achieving their demented goals, which included the elimination of the Jewish race and of all others whom Hitler considered "undesirable."

Among the undesirables that Hitler considered for genocide or slave labor were political enemies, including Communists, Trade Unionists, Anarchists, Liberals, Jehovah's Witnesses, Social Democrats, and members of other organized groups. People in these groups would be sent to concentration camps or ghettos. Once there, they would have to wear red triangles, pointed down, on their clothing. Blue triangles marked Slavs (mostly Poles and Russians) and many other immigrants who were now destined for slave labor.

An exception to the world turning a blind eye were members of the American Communist Party, who protested in Manhattan, NY, against Nazi policies on March 25, 1933.

Habitual criminals and convicts sent to camps wore green triangles; Jehovah's Witnesses and Seventh Day Adventists wore purple ones. Black triangles marked those deemed to be asocial elements and mentally retarded and handicapped individuals. Gypsies wore brown triangles; POWs, spies, and deserters wore red ones, pointed upward. There were also pink triangles, for homosexuals. Each Jew wore the six-pointed star along with a triangle if a triangle was appropriate.

PART II

Cloudy, Chance of rain!
1934–1935

Chapter 3

Jews are banned from labor unions.

Jews' health insurance is canceled.

Jews are banned from practicing any form of law.

All non-Nazi organizations are banned.

*Farmer unions, labor unions, church youth groups, and Boys and Girls Clubs
are all placed under Nazi control.*

Homosexual males are singled out for castration, prison, or death.

A broader definition of non-Aryans is implemented.

*Now, anyone with one or more Jewish parents or grandparents
is considered a Jew.*

Hitler's SA (*Sturm Abteilung*), also known as his storm troopers or the Brown Shirts, had outgrown its purpose in the Nazi Party and was now viewed as a threat to the party and its future. These storm troopers were anti-capitalist and anti-traditionalist; they wanted a second revolution and wanted to replace the regular German Army. Their Marxist inclinations were at loggerheads with the regular army and its traditions. The SA's Marxism also did not sit well with the big industry leaders, the manufacturing conglomerates, and the bankers. The old army generals wanted their old military privileges and traditions back. The generals supported breaking the Treaty of Versailles, which placed limits on the size of Germany's armed forces.

Those in the business sector also wanted the treaty thrown out so that they could sell products to the army to fill its growing needs. They wanted to achieve new economic growth, along with more freedom to trade than was currently allowed. They also wanted to toss out the Weimer Law that was passed by the Allies after WWI; they felt that this also was hindering growth and their ability to compete globally.

Hitler felt he needed the support of the regular army and big business if he wanted to stay in power, as well as to rearm. He desired new weapons so he could seize more land for his country and people. With new arms manufacturing there would also be job growth. The SA was considered a hindrance to this happening, and so it had to be reined in.

On June 30, 1934, Hitler put into action a plan called "The Night of the Long Knife." Special SS forces were armed with a list of SA leaders or Hitler's Brown Shirts (who actually comprised a group of well-trained troops) inside of the SS. These special SS forces, who were originally organized as personal bodyguards for Hitler, went out and murdered hundreds of leading SA members who were on the list.

By July 2, the killings were over, with the actual number of SA killed never known but estimated to be 150–200. Hitler had just elevated himself to supreme judge. This allowed him to choose, at his whim, who should be killed and who should be allowed to live. The SA became basically impotent and would soon be absorbed into the regular army. Some members of the SA were killed not over their political ideas but due to the fact that quite a few men in the organization were considered to be homosexual, including some of its highest leaders.

Germany had for many years had laws against sexual crimes, such as bestiality, rape, and pedophilia, and against homosexual conduct. Law 175 specifically spelled out that a man who had sex with another man would be arrested and jailed, and might be castrated or sent to a concentration camp. No specific punishment was ever put in place against lesbians; although lesbian sexual activity was considered illegal behavior, rarely was any punitive action enforced.

Passengers on a ship flee Germany; among them is W. Androndeus, who would lead a gay resistance group that bombed the Amsterdam Population Registry office in an effort to destroy government records of Jews and others sought by the Nazis. He was executed for his efforts shortly thereafter.

Hitler rewarded the SS for cleaning out the SA by making it independent from the SA and only answerable to Hitler himself. Its powers were greatly increased, and it would become Hitler's number one tool in his efforts to eliminate the Jewish population by mass murder.

On August 2, 1934, Germany's President Hindenburg died, following a lengthy period of illness. Hitler used the temporary powers the Enabling Act had given him. He abolished the office of the president and gave himself all of the powers the president's office had held. Hitler and his Nazi Party then announced a new law stating that the office of the president, along with all of its authority, would be combined with that of the chancellor, thus making Adolf Hitler the lone dictatorial power: the Führer of Germany.

Following this announcement, every public official and all members of the military were required to take an oath of loyalty to Hitler, in person. This elevated Hitler's powers, as now the armed forces were under his personal control. The Nazi Party even called for a vote of approval of Hitler's powers, and Hitler received 90% of the votes cast by about 95% of Germany's eligible voters. He was now the law as directed by the people.

The Jews were becoming the perpetual scapegoats, despised for simply being. *Jude* phobia was rampant, like a train barreling down a mountain without brakes. Individuals in the gentile populace were effectively enmeshed in Hitler's sadism, and they were unable to foresee the aftermath of their condoning such vengeance. So far, the Tauchers had escaped the violence and open hatred, and had felt only minor effects from all the new restrictions. They were content to get on with life and wait for this storm cloud to pass by, as it surely must.

The only thing Therese and Julius had known about the midwife they called to help with Fred's birth, Gertrude Nölting, was that she was obviously not Jewish. She was grandmotherly looking, yet determined. Her demeanor appeared stiff yet would also show compassion. Gertrude showed sincere concern and caring while participating in the birth, engendering Therese's warmth in return.

The old adage of not taking one at the first glimpse definitely applied to Gertrude, as there was a great deal about her life yet to be revealed. A lady of middle age, she lived with a younger woman by the name of Traute Holina whom all assumed to be her daughter. They also assumed Traute's father was a victim of war, which would account for his absence, a common situation after WWI, and could also account for the different last names.

There was even more to Gertrude than what had first met the parents' eyes, and it was slowly surfacing. They were startled by their new discovery about this helpful woman. They had discovered that she was a Nazi Party member. Pointedly, Gertrude was included among Adolf Hitler's friends and most loyal supporters in the years that he spent climbing toward his political ambitions.

She even had purchased a small summer cabin in the outskirts of Berlin among many of the higher ranking Nazis and SS officers. It was seemingly incomprehensible to the Tauchers that Mrs. Müller could have recommended Gertrude, if she had known this about her. Yet, there was absolutely no doubt that both ladies were fully aware they were helping a Jewish family.

Chapter 4

Jews are banned from the German military.

*A law is passed stating that to be a German all four
of one's grandparents must be of Aryan blood.*

Jews and non-Germans are stripped of their German citizenship.

*Jews are prohibited from marrying Germans, and annulment laws
for mixed marriages are passed.*

The Nazi swastika flag becomes the flag of Germany.

The term "Jude" officially replaces the term "non-Aryan."

*German females under the age of 45 are not allowed
to work in Jewish households.*

*Violation of any of these laws can result in imprisonment,
fines, hard labor, and even death.*

German Jewish passports can be used to exit the country but not to return.

A large "J" is stamped on all Jewish passports.

Jews are barred from public schools after age 14.

Public parks, libraries and beaches are closed to Jews.

The year 1935 was a busy one for Adolph Hitler, as he consolidated his powers and control over the Reich. His major goals were the elimination of the Jewish presence throughout the world and the expansion of the size of the German Reich. He started out the year with a major step toward his goal of expansion. In January, the citizens of an area that was formerly part of Germany but, as mandated by the Versailles Treaty, was then occupied and governed by the French and British had the opportunity to vote on its future.

This area, named Saarland, was a highly industrial area and held huge coal deposits. Under the treaty mandate, it was stipulated that after 15 years from the date of the treaty a plebiscite (vote) would be taken to determine this area's future. Most of the population of the Saar's region was ethnically German, with strong anti-French sentiments. On January 13, 1935, this region was returned to Germany after 90% of its voters voted to rejoin Germany. Hitler felt victorious for his Nazi Party and for himself as well.

Once the Saarland was returned to Germany by the League of Nations, Hitler promptly took Germany out of the League of Nations. Next, he basically abolished the Treaty of Versailles, which had always been one of his major aims. He began rearming Germany, which directly defied the terms of the treaty. He started building submarines, airplanes, and tanks. He also moved troops into the demilitarized zone along the Rhine River and reintroduced conscription. Both France and Britain adopted an appeasement policy toward Hitler's re-militarizing of the Rhineland.

German troops cross the Rhine River during the re-militarization of the Rhineland.

Now, with his expansionist goals coming to fruition and his war machine striving forward, Hitler turned his effort toward the Jewish population. During the year, the SS, the Gestapo, and the rest of the Nazis lashed out at the Jewish population with a wave of violent assaults, vandalism, and boycotts of businesses. Things became so bad that Hitler even ordered a halt to these individuals' behavior against the Jews, although only for a short time. The average German did not approve of this reckless behavior, although the police tolerated it. The German minister of economics also called for a halt to violence due to the Jewish entrepreneurial skills' large contributions to the economy.

Hitler and his party wanted harsh anti-Semitic laws passed that would define and allow such violence to continue, but in a legal manner. To achieve this, Hitler had the Reichstag (Parliament) moved to the town of Nürnberg, just in time for the annual Nazi Party rally. The rally had been held there yearly since 1925, but this was the first year in which the Reichstag convened there. Two measures came out of the rally and were passed into law shortly after by the Reichstag. These measures were to be known as the Nürnberg Laws and allowed anti-Semitic behavior to be legal and enforceable. Almost all of the restrictions and laws listed at the top of this chapter came out of these two laws.

The biggest change was that Judaism was now determined by ancestry and not by beliefs or practices. Many German citizens who had not practiced Judaism, did not identify themselves as Jewish, did not belong to the Jewish community, and in some cases even had converted to Christianity years ago were now defined by law as Jews. Besides institutionalizing many racist ideas, these new laws increased the Jewish population from an estimated 600,000 in all of Germany and 150,000 in Berlin in

1933, to possibly 2,500,000 in Germany and 500,000 in Berlin as of this decree in 1935.

It was now two years into Hitler's brutal governmental coalition, an operation that was hindering and threatening the lives and safety of the Jewish people. At this year's party rally, Hitler gave a spirited speech to a sizable crowd, detailing his unwavering hatred of Jews, uncaringly knowing full well that the reverberations would be heard around the world.

Gertrude Nölting was educated and intelligent, having even earned a midwife license. Her seemingly categorical absolution of Hitler's mastership of violence that was directed at so many people was puzzling. Quite extraordinary also were Mrs. and Mr. Taucher, who just brushed aside the red flag of Gertrude's admiration for Hitler. With good faith obscuring their reasoning, they believed that judging this nice lady solely on her close affiliation with such a vicious scoundrel was beneath them. They saw her as worthy of their respect, as she had only shown them kindness, appearing to truly value her closeness to the whole family.

Her daughter Traute also had her own allegiance to Nazism that would be rewarded with her appointment as an official photographer of the SS; among her duties would be taking photos of the achievements of the Nazi Party. Imagine the gruesome pictures she must have taken over the years, as the Germans made sure that everything was always thoroughly documented, especially in death.

Gertrude was a vision in contrast beyond a doubt, as if coated by many different hues. Yet, in spite of all the Tauchers knew, they remained trusting of her, believing that she would not pierce this veil of caring comradeship or bring any harm to their family. In reality, they had no choice but to ignore these warning signs. Their beliefs would be put to the ultimate test during the forthcoming years in unimaginable ways, as the family was repeatedly driven to seek assistance from these Nazi sympathizers, Gertrude and Traute. It's puzzling that the Tauchers never would perceive these two women as enemies whom they needed to avoid.

Cradled in the warmth of family togetherness, Hank, age three, and Fred, age two, could not comprehend the weakened roots beneath their feet. Their parents loved them to the sky, giving them all they needed as they soaked up the joys of toddlerhood. With faith affirmed, the parents' concerns were left at bay, and normalcy was maintained within their household, even under the relentless assault of the oppressive enemies, Hitler and his Nazis. Jews everywhere were trying to keep their lives steady amidst the spiraling repression and unbridled rancor that was causing them discomfort and foreshadowing their defenselessness.

Under the protection of home, Hank and Fred found pleasure in the company of their mother, who was a welcome playmate during their father's long hours of working in the shop. With food sparse and expensive, she was a natural at nourishing their spirits, feeding them through her positive outlook and understanding the need to reinforce their sense of self-worth. She always looked nice, even around the house, and always donned a hat when out in public to complete her ensemble.

A special time each day for the boys was their mother's reading to them before they went to sleep. Snuggling under the covers, they enthusiastically held their gaze upon her, lulled by her soothing voice, until the haven of slumber closed in and their dreams beckoned. Birthdays were celebrated with a freshly baked cake, and if Julius had an especially profitable month, he would buy them a toy. Fortunately, Therese was a terrific cook, magically creating tasty dishes from what little food could be afforded during these times of runaway inflation. The family would sit humbly together, savoring the few morsels set before them.

Hank and Fred were raised in a Reform setting, with any formal religious education minimal, yet their parents did traditionally observe various holy days. Hanukah, Passover, and Rosh Hashanah, among others, were always celebrated. The parents, wanting to instill a sense of meaning about their culture into the boys, honored the Sabbath with the family's weekly observances. After dinner on the Sabbath, they would step out into the pewter dusk and walk to the synagogue, three buildings away down the street. The services were conducted in Hebrew, since the synagogue was strictly Orthodox

For Hank and Fred, the highlight of the services came at the end, when they opened their lips for one sip of the ruby red wine that would warm their bodies, coating their feelings in lightness. Their parents began teaching the boys, from an early age, to be mindful of their rich heritage. They instilled in the boys the virtue of caring for others and taught them to believe in themselves and to value their faith. In the dark years to come, these principles would become immeasurably hard to hold on to and would repeatedly be put to the test.

Rosh Hashanah (Jewish New Year) was the only time of the year that Fred would get a few new clothes, not Hank's hand-me-downs. Julius gave Fred a new pair of pants that he had made, and parents and son all beamed with wide smiles. There was never much reason to celebrate during this era in Berlin. The family just accepted the things they could not change.

Gathering Storm Clouds!
1936–1937

Chapter 5

Having tossed out the Versailles Treaty, Hitler seriously cranked up his rearming of the German Army. He also sent 15,000 troops to Italy to help his role model, Mussolini, in the civil war there and to try out his new weapons. The production of arms greatly reduced unemployment. The German public was enthralled by this change from the dark days of the worldwide Depression that followed the end of WWI. Hitler got all the credit for bringing the German economy back to being one of the strongest in the world.

Since the late 1800s, Germany had built the world's largest and most modern train transportation system. Many of the train tracks and boarding platforms were built underground. Water, sewage and electrical lines were also placed in the tunnels. One of many notable stations was the Anhalter Bahnhof, which, in 1910, was considered the largest station on the European continent; it was a most magnificent and impressive structure. Above ground, the building could accommodate 40,000 travelers at a time, while thousands of arrivals and departures occurred below ground.

When Hitler took power, he needed to upgrade the train systems and other infrastructures for the Olympic Games, so the government hired thousands of workers to do the work. He also had the structures reinforced so that they could be used as bomb shelters and command posts. Also, large anti-aircraft flack gun towers were built nearby. The fact that so many trains could move around underground would later play an important role in the Battle of Berlin. The German people were thrilled with the job opportunities. Hitler was successful in hiding the true nature of the work from the German people.

The Summer Olympic Games were held in Berlin, and the Winter Games were held in Garmisch-Partenkirchen, Bavaria. This would be the last time one country would host both games in the same year. The Games were awarded to Germany in 1931, before the Nazis came into power. The Olympics of 1936 would become known as the Nazi Games.

The international community did discuss a possible boycott, due to the Nazis' control over Germany and their racist policies. The United States came very close to not sending its athletes but accepted the invitation to attend at the last minute.

Signs that had been posted throughout Berlin in shops and public places that proclaimed "Jews Unwelcome" were taken down,

Olympic Stamps issued by the Third Reich commendation of the 1936 Games.

and for a few weeks before and during the games, attacks against Jews were discouraged and were also greatly reduced. Gypsies continued to be rounded up and sent to camps, while at the same time Hitler ordered the relaxation of anti-homosexuality laws for visitors.

The Summer Games were elaborately staged, with four grandiose new stadiums, modern swimming pools, giant polo grounds, and the most modern Olympic Village in history. The games were the first to be televised, although only in Germany. The games were also the first in which results were telexed out to the world as they happened, and for the first time ever, there was a torch relay.

The Nazis used the games to portray Germany as a nation that had been reborn and that had dealt with the Depression better than any other nation in the world. Hitler enjoyed being in the spotlight, with the public attention and prestige that came with hosting the games.

The outside world was looking forward to the games even though the news was slowly spreading about the anti-Semitic vengeance of the German government. Jews were being transported to camps in droves, and many murders of the other unwanted were also taking place in Germany.

Many athletes in Germany and abroad wanted the games boycotted, but only a modicum of representatives would boycott the games. Jewish organizations pleaded with the international community to wake up to this crisis, and they fully anticipated a supportive response to their pleas. No influential leaders, capable of swift condemnation of and reprisals against Hitler's ruthless brutality, responded to the pleas for help. All efforts to evoke a response fell on seemingly ignorant, deaf ears.

Easily turning the tables to suit his strategy, Hitler appeased game participants and governments alike by implicating the media for lies and false propaganda. Pulling the wool over all eyes by this whitewashing of the credible unfolding events, he convinced skeptics to squash any plans for interference, such as boycotts.

The games went off as scheduled, with neither race nor religion supposedly an issue. Hitler would not allow German Jews to compete, and he was appalled by the success of the black male athletes from the United States, especially Jesse Owens, who won four gold medals.

The USA's black athletes voted among themselves and chose to attend the games, thinking that black victories would undermine the Nazis' view of white supremacy, while Jewish groups opposed any attendance. Jesse Owens turned out to be the star of the Summer Games. Hitler did not like blacks but had no campaign directed toward them at this time. Jesse even found he had more freedom in Germany at this time then he had in the US. He was freely allowed to ride public transportation, and he entered bars and restaurants with less difficulty than he had back home.

Much ado was made about Hitler not shaking the winning black athletes' hands, but the truth is that after the first day of events, the IOC had warned him to start showing Olympic neutrality. He had shaken hands with only the German winners on day one, but after the warning, he just didn't shake any athlete's hand for the remainder of the games, German or otherwise.

American athletes arrive at the Olympic Village in Berlin flanked by German officers.

The US sent its team because the Olympics' creed states that one should not let politics interfere with the Games. Hitler did allow anyone qualified to enter, except in the case of his own team, from which all Jews and other "undesirables" were banned. A few athletes from other countries elected to sit out, while their teams went ahead and played.

In all, 3,600 athletes from 49 nations, including for the first time Costa Rica, participated in 29 events in 19 sports at the Summer Games. Basketball was played for the first time as an Olympic medal sport. Its gold medal match was played outdoors, and the championship game was between Canada and the USA. A thousand people stood around the court in a driving rainstorm. The court was so muddy that the ball was never dribbled, and the US won by a score of 19-8. The American team from the University of Washington won the eight-man team rowing event over the Germans and Italians while Hitler watched; he was not amused.

The Winter Games also took place in Germany in this same year, but the world seemed not to notice. There were no protests, nor was there the grandiose staging by the Nazis that was present at the Summer Games. In all, 28 nations participated in 17 events, in 4 sports. Hitler did attend, only to watch Norway easily win the games, with Germany a distant second.

Immediately after the Summer Games, the Nazis once again stepped up their persecution of the Jewish population. The world did not know it then, but the Olympic Games would not take place for the next 12 years due to the coming of WWII. Already into the third year of their reign of terror, the Nazis resumed the terror by conducting home invasions, ceaselessly committing murder, and arresting Jewish people and herding them off to concentration camps in huge numbers. The Jews' surreptitious disappearance was happening at an alarming rate, under the gentile radar, in the shadow of darkness. Hitler now proclaimed that anyone found to have any Jewish blood as far back as three generations was Jewish and now the target of his insanity. The Reichstag approved this new definition.

Jews and gentiles no longer shopped at the same markets, waved to each other in the parks, or shared meals. Most Germans felt it was best to just pretend not to see their old Jewish friends, to make believe they were invisible. This was done by both Jews and gentiles to avoid possible repercussions to all. Jews could no longer be productive members of society. Jewish fathers and mothers, decent and tranquil, were forbidden from showing their love of country, and their children were confused by contradictory visions. Over the next three years, Hitler continued his obsessive buildup of concentration camps, which were scattered across the country. The German people became spectators, watching cities and townships depreciate.

The perilous condition of the Taucher family's welfare rested squarely on Julius's shoulders, as he was the father. It took every ounce of his energy for him to set this burden aside and concentrate on the work at hand, but he was also smart enough not to ignore what loomed ahead. Therese could do little to make him feel better, and the boys were too young and were unwilling to give up their childhood.

Their rambunctious behavior was admittedly a distraction. Only a year apart, the boys were tight, though their contrasting personalities caused a certain degree of sibling rivalry. When peaceful, they played checkers or cards and kicked around an old ball, their substitute for a soccer ball. Other times they would be at each other's throats, like cats and dogs, but would eventually settle their differences without lingering resentment.

The father, as the authoritarian, always maintained high expectations for the children's behavior in the company of elders, with no time for tomfoolery. In his day, the slant of child development that advocates that kids be kids was less common; instead, the slant was that children should be seen and not heard. The boys loved their father, but as much as they tried to be quiet, his growing impatience with their sporting about unintentionally landed them in his disfavor many times. Early on, Hank's aggressiveness showed up, and he would stubbornly speak out of turn. Looking up to Hank in admiration, Fred would envy his spunk and his rebellious disposition.

But Julius was finding it hard to appreciate how childhood fears might be the source of Hank's behavior. With the pressures of keeping the family safe and sound, he knew that much of his own distress needed to remain under wraps, yet with anti-Semitic fury so infectious, he was sometimes filled with a rage that would every once in a while become uncontrollable. With words having failed and Hank's display for attention forcing Julius to rage, Therese would step in and get things under control quickly, with no harm being done. Fred was luckier; he inadvertently learned from Hank that less aggression is most effective when fending off those who might otherwise be prone to overreact.

Chapter 6

Jews are required to register their business properties.

Jewish doctors are not allowed to give treatment to non-Jews.

Jewish workers and managers are dismissed from all public and private employment except work related to the war preparations.

A law is passed that all German women must do one "Duty Year."

Jews are banned from teaching German students or practicing dentistry.

Jews are forbidden to touch money.

German bombers are sent to Italy, as are battleships, and both see action.

The Buchenwald concentration camp is completed and will operate until 1945.

Hitler tells his military staff, "We are going to war."

A law that all chimney sweepers must be German is approved, allowing for domestic spying.

Hitler eyed the bordering countries as potential targets that could fulfill his desire to expand Germany's area. Any army general, minister, or member of the general staff who opposed going to war and expansionism was promptly dismissed or just plain vanished. In November of 1937, Hitler held a conference in Berlin, with all of his top military aides. This conference, dubbed the "Führer Conference" was where he laid out his plans for war in Europe. He hated Marxists, Communists, Slavs, Social Democrats, blacks, gays, Gypsies, and Jews. He wanted all people of the Aryan race united under one single nation's banner. He believed all other races were inferior.

His rearming was going strongly ahead. Other nations remained silent, not complaining about Germany's violation of the treaty, although some countries were now gearing up their own production of arms and the numbers of their troops. It was slowly becoming apparent that Hitler wanted war and that a response to the seemingly growing war clouds would be necessary.

Unemployment was at an all-time low in Germany and strong nationalistic sentiments were sweeping the country. The largest segment supporting Nazism was the lower middle class and peasants. They praised Hitler for turning the economy around. This segment was largely Protestant, while the Catholic segment stayed loyal to their Catholic Center Party, who cast their electoral votes with the Social Democrats. The Catholic Pope even met with Hitler's representative, Herman Göering, to see if the Nazis would moderate their campaign against the Jews.

Jews were flocking out of Germany at an increasing rate, getting out by any means possible, some legal and some not. The number that left rose from 37,000 in 1937 up to a high of 78,000 in 1939. The biggest problem was the cost of a visa, which had to be paid to the German government. There was also the difficulty of finding a host country that would accept them. The law stating that Jews were not allowed to touch money was ignored and never fully implemented.

This was happening not in just Germany but in countries all across Europe, as Jews everywhere began fleeing in anticipation of the Nazis' spreading influence. Over half of Austria's Jews were trying to flee from there, many paying huge amounts for a visa. Austria's Jewish population would drop from 250,000 to 135,000 in just a few years. Sigmund Freud escaped Austria only to die in England, partially from the stress of his escaping. Baron Louis Rothschild allegedly paid the Nazis $12,000,000 to allow him to leave.

Therese had a brother, Alfred, who was a dentist, and he immigrated to Shanghai before 1930. Therese's younger sister Rosl would follow, getting out of Germany just as Hitler was hitting hard on the new cultural movements that were occurring in Berlin, which he did not approve of. Rosl was an opera singer, with a theatrical flair that the Tauchers deemed inappropriate in a lady, but she too had gotten out of Germany before Hitler took power, and she would entertain the Jewish community in Shanghai for the entire duration of WWII.

The sad thing was that most Jews in Europe did not have enough readily available cash to escape. In Germany, they couldn't sell their businesses, as the Nazis would just cheat them out of the money or confiscate it. The

Theresia Seibel, who was from a Gypsy family and who performed in the Wuerzburg Stadttheater, personifies the cultural movement in Berlin during this period. Her family suffered dearly during the Nazi era, enduring torture, imprisonment, death, and medical experimentations. Special attention was paid to her twin daughters by Dr Mengele.

Tauchers looked at all means available to raise the funds necessary to find freedom outside of Germany. They quickly realized that there was no way the entire family could leave, but they hoped they could get Fred and Hank out to England. Regrettably, after weighing the excessive price demanded by the German government for two visas, they determined that the purchase price was definitely beyond the accrual of their family wealth. There was also no one that they knew who could be asked for help, as things were tight among all the people they knew.

Hitler's personal physician at this time was Dr. F. Sauerbruch, who stated "that Hitler is either a genius or is insane; possibly he is the craziest criminal the world has ever seen." Needless to say, the doctor was sent away, not to be heard from again.

When Hitler first came to power in 1933, one of the first things he did was to put into place the Nazis' position on the role of women in Germany. They were supposed to be good mothers, bring up a house full of children, and provide a good home for their husbands so they could work and produce. They should get married at a young age and have as many children as possible; Hitler even provided loans to newlyweds of 1,000 German marks, which were to be paid back by bearing children. For every child that a couple produced, 25% of the debt was forgiven; have four and no more debt. Almost a million newlyweds took Hitler up on the offer.

The Nazi leadership saw the future need for more soldiers to fight, which in turn required more mothers to keep up the supply of children: more men to fight and more women to have the needed babies. Also, the need was arising to populate the new lands that were to be conquered in Eastern Europe with pure Aryan blood. Unmarried women were even encouraged to have children for the cause. Hitler went as far as opening up places where women could go to get pregnant by racially pure SS men. These "clinics" were not hidden on backstreets; in fact, they were openly advertised. Many women took up the offer, and even more men volunteered for this patriotic duty.

Germany's women were encouraged not to wear makeup and not to wear high heels or trousers. Also discouraged were perms or the dying of hair. Being plump was encouraged. Every August, on Hitler's mother's birthday, he would award the Motherhood Cross to German women. Those with eight or more children received a gold cross, while a silver cross was given to those with six children, and a bronze one to those with four.

In 1937, the Nazis saw that with the likelihood of a large scale war there was a labor shortage. So a new law was passed that all women had to do a "Duty Year." The need for skilled workers in the factories was such that it was deemed the patriotic duty of women to work for at least one year, and the marriage loan program was suspended, as well as the fertility clinics.

A Storm Erupts: 1938–1939

Chapter 7

All Jewish properties, now both personal and business,
must be registered with the Reich.

Germany captures Austria without bloodshed or even firing a gun.

At the Evian Conference, only the Dominican Republic
agrees to accept more refugees.

The laws of Nazi Germany are applied in Austria.

Hitler has the Sudetenland of Czechoslovakia ceded to Germany.

Jews are not allowed to own a pet or a radio.

Most sweet treats such as ice cream and pastries are placed off limits to Jews.

Jews' driver licenses are canceled. Jews are not allowed to use public transportation.

Kristallnacht, the "Night of Pandemonium," takes place in Germany,
Poland, Austria, Hungary, and Czechoslovakia.

Nazis implement plans for all major cities in Germany and
its occupied lands to contain Jewish ghettos.

Berlin is sectioned into Jew and Jew-free areas.

A strict curfew for Jews is established, 8PM–5AM.

Hitler set in motion his plans to expand German territory and to bring all German-speaking descendants under one political roof. He started out in his homeland of Austria. In early 1938, Hitler issued a demand to the Austrian chancellor that the Nazi Party be represented in Austria's government. The chancellor resisted but changed his mind when a million German troops massed on the Austrian-German border. In March, the German troops crossed the border unopposed, taking Austria without firing a shot. Austria was declared a province of

Germany, and no other government in the world at this time voiced any objections.

In April of this year, a vote was held in Austria, and Austrian voters overwhelmingly chose to become part of Germany. Hitler was ecstatic and returned to his native Austria. The persecution of the Jews of Austria began immediately, with over half fleeing right away. Also, anyone who had objected to the Nazi regime was imprisoned and sent away to the concentration camps.

President Franklin D. Roosevelt called together 32 countries to address the issue of the mounting numbers of people who were seeking shelter from the Nazis and were applying to immigrate to any country that would accept them. Many excuses were offered, and much sympathy was expressed, but no solution was agreed upon. At this time, most Jews wanted to go to the US but

How blind? In 1938 the United States sent a track and field team to Germany for a "friendly" competition in the Olympic stadium.

were willing to go anywhere to escape alive. The Evian Conference was a failure.

Next, Hitler set his sights on Czechoslovakia, eyeing its highly industrialized Sudetenland region, which was heavily populated by German descendants. The Germans of this region resented living under Czechoslovakian control; they wanted autonomy. Amazingly, once again the world powers turned their backs to any alarms being voiced by a few concerned governments; instead, they chose to appease Hitler and just did not get involved. Nation after nation all stood down to Hitler's demands for the Sudetenland, and he finally took it in exchange for his not declaring a full-out invasion. Everyone who was involved in the long sessions and multiple negotiations held on this subject just went home afterward and began preparations for the seemingly inevitable war in Europe.

The year 1938 was the fifth year of Hitler's domination and of the proliferation of mandates driving European Jews into impoverishment. The glory of the hunt was in abolishing the Jews' presence and in devouring their flesh. The Third Reich's stealthy intention was, first, to eliminate the Jews of Europe. The Nazis murdered aplenty, thieving the Jews' hard-won prosperity, then turning everything over to the gentiles at a bargain price.

Thereafter, Jews were required to register the value of both their personal and business assets with German authorities, under the threat of criminal prosecution; the ultimate intimidation was death. Sure enough, Mr. Taucher got his notification in regard to his tailor shop and the worth of all of the family's personal belongings. Naturally, Julius dutifully registered his properties.

Julius could not shake his panic over the likely loss of his business and the darkened hopes for his family. Hardly allowing any time for a meal or for rest, he was encumbered with overwhelming responsibility. The family naturally felt sorry that they could not help him in what now had become an extremely difficult situation. Their regard for his strength and tireless concern for their welfare never faltered. There were few happy moments; wherever they could catch one, they would hold it tight.

The family let down their guard in their excitement for Hank and his important milestone—entering first grade—and they all anticipated the start of his classes in the fall of 1938, with Hank looking forward to making new friends as much as to learning his subjects. At last the day arrived, and the Tauchers wore smiles to conceal their jitters, immensely proud to see their firstborn off to school.

Therese had worked very hard to find a school where Hank could study. The German public school system was no longer accepting Jewish children. This measure was enforced to relieve the overcrowded public school systems but fell far short of addressing the problem. Many German parents had even already turned to the Hitler Youth Organization to train and school their sons and daughters; the organization turned out thugs and no scholars.

The few German Jewish schools still open were suffering from extreme overcrowding, with long waiting lists of applicants now the norm. Most openings were due to families fleeing the hostilities or just simply choosing not to send their children to school amidst the violence that they could encounter. The Jewish students suffered horrible encounters with bullying youths, who would intercept them when they were coming and going to school. Most of the handful of schools still open had to cancel outside recesses, as the children were targets of rock-throwing punks. The principals and teachers were powerless over this violence, as a Nazi political overseer placed in each school would deem the violence insignificant. Racial slogans that appeared on walls near the schools were a common reminder of hatred as the students walked to classes.

Owning a radio had been forbidden to Jews for a while, so they talked with their gentile neighbors, who secretly informed them of all that was transpiring. The German government had taken control of the radio stations by this time, so not a lot of the truth was broadcast. The reality of being numbered amongst the hundreds of thousands of Jews in direct jeopardy was chilling. In truth, the number threatened would rise to about 5 million before the end of the war. The Nazis clearly were hounding them like vultures, and the same question was heavy on the minds of all Jews: how much longer before the Nazis' sheer cruelty would totally encroach upon their families?

Now, new orders were issued making invalid all driver licenses held by Jews, and toward the end of the year the Nazis also began cracking down on the Jews' use of public transportation, stating that they could only use it for war-related employment. Although the Tauchers had never had a car, they had fond memories of going on daily outings before this latest prohibition, to buy a few groceries or perhaps just to take a ride on a streetcar to the next town for ice cream. All of these little pleasures were now off-limits.

The Tauchers never could afford to keep a pet, nor were Jews allowed to own one. They did share a love for animals and would occasionally take a walking excursion to one of the world's greatest zoos, the Berlin Zoologischer Garten. Wonderstruck by so much of the animal kingdom in one place, they would stay several hours before heading home, their life feeling perfect as they shared these times together. The boys felt truly fortunate to have down-to-earth parents, who made up for the limitations on such adventures by engaging in easy conversations. The whole family gained a broader knowledge about animals and the beauty of nature, about the arts and sciences, and about different cultures and the associational dynamics of all living beings. More than simply a method of education, these outings gave the family moments in which to reflect and rejoice as well as a profound accentuation of the value of their presence amidst all the chaos in the world.

The Tauchers most assuredly were seeing their days of ease numbered. On November 4, 1938, Julius went to open the shop and found the storefront window scrawled on with anti-Semitic graffiti. Here again, it seemed like it was years earlier, when Hitler's rants could be heard booming from loudspeakers around Berlin, inciting gentiles to boycott Jewish-owned businesses in anticipation of their expected closures.

Julius recognized that this filth was meant to deter business, but he decided not to make a big deal about the mess and ignored it for the moment. But the next day the Gestapo was at the door and, perceiving defiance, rebuked Julius strongly, ordering his prompt cleaning of this Nazi filth. He did the best he could and, in doing so, he hoped that if he appeased their demands they might allow him to keep his shop, though realistically he sensed that it would be taken soon.

Julius remained steadfast even under duress, showing the boys how a man's character is the essential determinant of his forward progress. Judaism's teaching of nonviolence is an attestation of its civility. Yet one human can take only so much provocation before retaliating. These tempestuous times, especially, called for extreme discipline, as any reaction could unduly place you at risk of arrest or death.

One of the most violent nights in history soon followed, in November of 1938. It occurred after Germany asked Poland to accept 50,000 Polish Jews that Germany wanted to ship back to Poland, whether they wanted to go or not. Poland refused, so Germany loaded up 3,000 of them and sent them by boxcar to the German-Polish border. Poland refused to let them enter, and there they sat for three days in terrible conditions. Finally, they were allowed across the border into Poland and were placed in a livestock corral where they received their first food and water in days.

When word of their treatment became known, a young Polish Jew in Paris, who actually heard about the incident from a relative who had been on the train, took things into his own hands. He went to the German Embassy in Paris and shot a relatively unimportant German diplomat, injuring him superficially. The diplomat, who just happened to not be anti-Semitic, was attended by French doctors and appeared to be recovering. Then German doctors came and took over, the diplomat got promoted, and then he mysteriously died. The German public was livid at the Polish Jews and started attacking anything Jewish. The whole thing may well have been fully orchestrated, but it was surely the end for this lowly official, who left behind a legacy that he certainly did not want.

The Night of Broken Glass, *Kristallnacht*, erupted on November 9. In just one night in Germany, Austria, Poland, and elsewhere hundreds of Jews were murdered, thousands of synagogues were burned, and thousands of Jewish businesses and homes were destroyed.

Over 30,000 of Berlin's Jews were rounded up and shipped to concentration camps. Looting took place at every Jewish home and business that could be identified. Jews were beaten and killed, while others were made to clean up the mess. Many Jews just killed

Newly arrived prisoners, heads shaven, stand at roll call at Buchenwald concentration camp. Among them are 10,000 of the more than 30,000 Berlin Jews who were arrested.

themselves, seeing no hope. Insurance claims for the damage were paid, only to be diverted by the Nazis for their own use. Many more Jews now began trying to emigrate to anywhere they could, but by now most doors were shut tight with little hope of unlocking them.

The boys were not quite six and seven years old, but this event is lodged in their memories forever. In the pre-dawn hours, jolted out of their sleep, they heard the terrible sound of glass shattering down, from all around. Nazi villains were ransacking their family's personal sanctum, snatching up the clothing inventory and works in progress, wrecking the sewing machine and pressing irons. Gone were almost all of the tools precious to a tailor, and their home was left all but completely destroyed. Time and space froze, their thoughts raced; they dared not approach the perpetrators. How could these people take away everything that Julius had worked so hard to achieve? "Are they going to kill us? Help us God!"

This was the start of the historic *Kristallnacht*, which can be translated as, "night of broken crystal glass." Crystal glass refers to the high quality glass used in shops' storefronts and only available from Austria. Germany was in absolute chaos, and the Jews were paralyzed and restrained from action. Over two days and nights, the Gestapo and SS stormed Jewish residences and cold-bloodedly killed people as they slept or attempted escape. The Nazis, as if trying to hit their quota, were perversely satisfied in the taking of these defenseless lives, while businesses were being demolished.

The streets were soon covered with broken glass for miles around; Judaic literature and all other publications authored by Jews were thrown into bonfires; synagogues, where once the sacred Torah scrolls had been protected, were now set ablaze; and smoke billowed into the night sky, choking the atmosphere. Other countries were also soon in absolute chaos, with Jews paralyzed and restrained from action.

Just three buildings down the street from the Tauchers' tailor shop, their synagogue was among those gutted by the ravenous flames. After that, one of the neighbors opened his house for services. Despite the increased danger of capture, the Tauchers and many like them preferred to congregate somewhere. It seemed that all that was left for them to do was to pray with all their might for a miracle to occur.

This pogrom was the first of many that happened in quick succession: an organized mutilation of whole towns in Germany, which spread across the borders. The Jews were being submerged in a virtual quagmire, yet politicians' opposition elicited only a perfunctory response. There were no economic sanctions or changes in diplomacy, nor was any other formal position taken to curtail Hitler's behavior. The free world responded by remaining unobservant.

Hitler's next strategy to permanently remove the Jewish people from Europe was to have thousands more arrested and then forced onto trucks and trains bound for the ghettos and holding camps. Thousands more were transported directly to the many recently built concentration camps in Germany, Poland, Hungary, Austria, and other sites across the European continent. Yet to be constructed on these sites were the actual extermination apparatuses that would soon be up and running within the next two years. Hitler ordered this construction to be done as quickly as possible, as his soldiers were suffering from low morale from all the shooting of prisoners they had been doing.

For a brief time, many Jewish prisoners not mortally injured were released, on the sole condition of their surrendering all valuables; thereupon, the Nazis provided documentation allowing for their emigration. This definitely appeared to be their last opportunity to save their own skins, but in all reality the offer was made under false pretenses. Most never were released or, if released, were quickly rearrested.

Hank and Fred, although still so very young, heard of the arrest of many store owners in their neighborhood. Many were acquaintances or close friends of their family. When the assaults and pillaging moved out of the cities, it spread into the countryside, and then returned to the cities, while the Nazis gleefully viewed the destruction.

When the Nazis returned to the family shop, they interrogated Julius as if he himself had wrecked his own shop. They warned him: "Sweep up the shattered glass and fix your property within 48 hours." Of course, the repairs would be at his expense, but the family's deathly fears of his being apprehended on the spot were allayed. Julius did his best with the windowpane damage, putting up boards, since the cost to replace glass was beyond his means. In his sullen eyes, his spirit could be seen to be visibly shaken, yet he vowed to keep his business afloat and to serve his loyal customers one way or another.

Julius's escape from arrest was indeed a narrow one and may have been due to the fact that he was once an American citizen, having been born in New York City, or because he had been in the German Army during WWI. His family would never know for sure, but Julius was fast becoming acutely cognizant of the Nazis' affinity toward cruelty and sensed they were toying with his mind, presaging future belligerence. The family could only count their blessings, never knowing really who to give thanks to.

By the day and hour, luck was running out. For this moment, at least, they felt tremendously grateful that Julius was still free. Therese's distressed sigh of relief summed it up while they all wrapped their arms around Dad, in silent supplication. Therese was heard asking, "What are we going to do now? Who is going to pay for all that has been destroyed of the shop and the vocation you have so loved?" Julius took a moment before responding with calm assurance, "We have an insurance policy that covers this kind of loss." At the time, they did not know that no claims for reimbursement would ever reach the Jewish population because all payments would be stolen by the Nazis. Julius did his best to clean up the mess.

The success of the pogrom gave the Nazis the courage to take Hitler's desire for a Jewish-free Europe forward. Even though the average German citizen basically drew his window blinds closed to the violence, knowing it was probably in his best interest to ignore the destruction caused mostly by the Nazis, the SS, the Gestapo, and street punks, many were thoroughly disgusted by what was happening to their Jewish neighbors.

Finally, on November 12–13, 1938, a confident Hitler placed most of Berlin off-limits to Jews. Jews now were allowed to live

View of the Allianz insurance company in Berlin in 1931, before the Nazi influence was felt and while Berlin was still a beautiful place to live.

in only a few small areas. Movement near these areas was strictly monitored, and passes were required for Jews to come and go. Suddenly, families and shop owners were forced to move, always to where they were told to.

The lucky ones of Berlin were allowed to pack a few belongings, usually only a few changes of clothing, and were assigned to a run-down apartment building in one of the newly established Jewish zones. Many weren't so lucky; in Berlin alone, thousands were rounded up and simply hauled off to concentration camps. Once there, they were subjected to the Nazis' brutality; most would only survive long enough to be shipped to their deaths at the Auschwitz death camp, while others were put to slave labor.

Germans and their families were, at the same time, being moved out of these Jewish areas, as soon as other housing opened for them elsewhere, mostly in the homes and shops that the Jews had been forced to abandon. The Tauchers did what so many others were doing: waited for that knock on the door, which, when opened, would inevitably reveal a Nazi officer with a notice to prepare to move.

Strangely, the Tauchers watched while their neighborhood was mostly emptied of all their Jewish neighbors during the next two months. Soon they were among the few remaining Jews on their block. Julius didn't know what to do as they were not allowed on their street. He couldn't dare go out to find any information, as he did not wish to draw any attention. The Tauchers wondered if someone had slipped and they had been forgotten, or if Gertrude somehow had a hand in it. Not knowing was weighing heavily on them.

The wait turned out to be short, as the knock finally came. Julius was told that he must close the tailor shop and move the family to a new location, located just a few blocks away at Leiebnitzstraße 27. Their new home had a shop, with a living area: it was very small, and it had only one bedroom and no kitchen. The bathroom and plumbing were all outdoors. The family had lost all the items that they had considered luxuries at their previous location. Although there were still Germans living in the area with the Jews, Hitler was moving them out as fast as he could. Julius was puzzled but happy that somehow he still had a place to work, although he had few tools, no inventory, and only a little furniture.

Once they moved, things became very terrifying, as they were now really feeling the wrath of the Nazis, living as they did in a part of Berlin that was in the worst ghetto and under the wrathful watch of the Nazis' radar. The Tauchers' freedoms dissolved.

Therese had been doing a little part-time work at a gentile laundry that was owned by a lady known as Mrs. Müller, near to where the Tauchers had lived. Mrs. Müller arranged for a permit for Therese so that she could continue working at her laundry. Mrs. Müller was not allowed to pay her Jewish workers any money, but she could give them small items such as soap or some food. She would slip her workers some money or ration cards when she had some available. She also was the one who had introduced Therese to Gertrude, who was Fred's midwife.

Mrs. Müller was one of those good Germans. Some Germans would just find a Jew and make them work and not pay them, as this treatment was allowed and preferred by the Nazis. Berlin always had some anti-Nazism in it, but the average German either chose to ignore what was going on or was too frightened to speak out. The Night of Broken Glass had not been very popular among many Berliners, as they saw many friends and popular shop owners' lives and businesses destroyed; only the trash of Hitler's followers were overjoyed by that event.

Therese's son Klaus from her previous marriage also knew Mrs. Müller and would arrange to meet Therese at the laundry. He would always bring a small gift with him for his half brothers. In 1937, he had been arrested by the Nazis and shipped to the concentration camp at Buchenwald. Somehow he had gotten himself released under the understanding that he had only 90 days to get himself out of Germany. Sadly, he wasn't able to come up with the necessary funds to purchase an exit visa from the Nazis.

With no other option, he went into hiding in Berlin before his time ran out. Upon learning where he was living, the Nazis came to his apartment to arrest him, on March 9, 1938. He chose death over going back to a concentration camp and the sure slow death that would await him there as he slaved for his tormentors. Klaus, seeing the Nazis approach, leaped down the spiral staircase at his apartment, committing suicide. Therese did manage to arrange for his burial at a Jewish cemetery in Berlin, called Weissensee. Many Jews were, at that time, committing suicide to avoid arrest, even though this was against their religious beliefs.

Klaus was not Therese's only loss. A sister, Hanne Putzrath, was married to a non-Jew, who was paralyzed and in a wheelchair. This would eventually lead to arrests and jail sentences for both of them, as Hitler hated Jews and would not tolerate handicapped persons. The Hereditary laws gave him the power to have them eliminated.

Chapter 8

*Jews are forbidden from working, except in the armament
and other war-related industries.*

Jewish jewelry is confiscated, as are Jewish homes.

Clothing and food rations are canceled or reduced for Jews.

Jews are allowed to shop only at certain stores during certain hours.

World War II begins when Germany invades Poland.

Canada declares war against Germany.

Hitler proclaims he will rid Europe of all Jews.

Germany launches air attacks on Great Britain.

Homosexuals are rounded up; most will die in camps.

Soap and other hygiene products are placed off-limits to Jews.

The Third Reich's intensifying savagery was furthering the isolation of the Jews from the rest of German society. This year, 1939, began with the expulsion of Jews from most public schools and all universities, as well as from patronage at restaurants and entertainment and sport venues. Signs prohibiting them, which displayed the ultimate expression of abundant loathing—No <u>Jews</u> or <u>Dogs</u> Allowed—were hung all around.

At the start of summer in 1939 came the mandate that Jews must not possess any products necessary for personal hygiene; every last such item was to be immediately discarded. As much as the numerous prior restrictions dehumanized them, this one cut to the heart of their pride. Hitler wanted the Jews to be fixed in squalor, to propagate irrational images amongst the gentiles of Jews that were filthy and disgusting, and thus deserving of condemnation. Jews who were so unkempt would stand out and be easy targets. Posters were posted throughout Germany proclaiming <u>NO Soap to Jews</u>.

Therese had always taken pride in her family's cleanliness and tidy clothing. A shop must have a clean appearance, as must the owner and the owner's family. This new restriction tore at the heart of her being; it was completely unacceptable to her. She turned to the only source of help she knew, her gentile friends. Gertrude would and did secretly help to supply the Tauchers with soap and other things, as did Mrs. Müller. Therese had always maintained a well-kept family and would not abide by the rules and allow her family to be unclean.

After having lived at the apartment-shop on Leibnizstraße 27 for a little more than a year, the Tauchers received a notice to be prepared to move once again. Now that the family was relegated to deeper within one of the worst ghetto areas in Berlin, the Nazi net was growing ever so tight. They were given a list of items that they could take with them, and anything else was to be nicely boxed for "storage." They were permitted a minimum of personal items, and now had to part with the few other items they had managed to hold on to. It was painful knowing that their meager belongings would in reality be going to some Nazi's household. No moving truck was required, nor were there any funds for one. With just two small cardboard boxes and a suitcase, the family took the short walk to the designated ghetto apartment building.

The new address was Kommandantenstraße 63/64. This multistory building was operated by the Nazis and had surely been confiscated by them from a Jewish owner. The building was now extremely run-down and overcrowded. There was one family allowed per room and many families on each floor. There was only one gas burner for cooking per floor, no refrigerators, and only outside plumbing. It was the worst living conditions they had ever experienced or probably ever even imagined in their worst nightmares. Totally grim at best, the one saving grace was that it was still within walking distance to Mrs. Müller's laundry.

Once again, Julius was not arrested, but he was now forced into slave labor. Wherever the Nazis required hard labor, like for repairing or building train tracks, slave labor was used. Soon the air raids would start, and the bulk of the work would be in

Prisoners doing forced labor on a railroad line.

repairing the resultant damage. The Nazis would come to the ghetto gates to take Julius and scores of other Jews to numerous work sites. As far as the Nazis were concerned, Julius, with his robust physique, was deemed satisfactory for slave labor.

Hitler also had engineered the construction of a highly intricate rail system outside of Berlin. A myriad of tracks wove to and from concentration camp sites in and out of Germany. The majority of trains were destined for Poland, where the greatest number of Jews would wind up, thus assuring swift and effective transport of the hundreds of thousands who were trapped inside these cattle cars. The tracks were also heavily used to move troops and their supplies and to facilitate arms production.

Julius was assigned to a labor checkpoint about five miles distant, where most of the time he would be dispatched to some rails nearby in need of repairs. Usually, a truck would pick up workers at the ghetto gate in the early morning and return them late at night, many hours later, seven days a week. Workers had better catch their ride, as no excuses were accepted. To be seen as too sick, weak, or injured to work would get you deemed worthless and sent to a camp to be killed. The Nazis figured that if you were useless to them, then it was better that you were dead.

The labor was arduous, and their bodies were worked to exhaustion from very early morning until late at night; guards toted guns at the ready and menacingly scrutinized their every move. If the Nazis observed one being indolent or ineffective in servitude to their vulgar expectations, that would be the end of him. Infuriated at being ripped from the bosom of his family, Julius was determined not to accept defeat. As long as he had control of his mind and body, he would put every ounce of his might into this grueling task, with little food or water, day after day, in powerless fury. His will, steadfast under the strain, refused these Nazis any indulgence.

When finally released at the witching hour, Julius would get back home, but he did not sleep much. Having grabbed up a few tailoring essentials at their last shop before the Nazis destroyed it, he concentrated on working on the sly for a bit of pay. With his nimble fingers busy, he would be less inclined to think, and not thinking helped to keep the madness at bay. If he was ever caught having these tools, his death would have been quick.

Occasionally, Therese would ask Mrs. Müller for some small item that Julius needed and could not procure elsewhere, to finish some tailoring. Out of the blue, one day Mrs. Müller asked Therese if Julius wanted to bring his tools over to her shop. She thought it would be in the best interest of the family to not have them at the apartment, where they would cause much trouble if discovered by the authorities.

He would then keep most of his tools at Mrs. Müller's laundry and would go over there under cover of darkness. He would not have to sneak out from the ghetto area. Mrs. Müller obtained an ID card for him that allowed Julius to go to the laundry, under the pretence that some heavy work needed to be done. She was taking great risk in helping him. The strain on him was visibly noticeable, but the blessing of his return each day, however brief, left the family contented.

The Skies Let Loose: Late 1939–1941

Chapter 9

All Jews must register at the Labor Ministry.

Jews are not allowed to purchase coffee.

Typewriters and sewing machines must be turned in.

Norway and France surrender.

*The Nazis loot Paris and Hitler personally views
the Eiffel Tower and other sights.*

The Auschwitz concentration camp opens.

Jews are not allowed on the street after 8PM in winter and 9PM in summer.

Church bells are melted down to be used in weapons production.

Jews can no longer own carrier pigeons.

Therese was now going to make sure Fred started first grade, and she sought to enroll him in the nearest school still open in the Jewish zone that would also allow Hank to advance to his second year of schooling. This would not be an easy task, as the very few choices were already overcrowded and had long waiting lists. Therese's tenacity regarding her sons' well being was once again put to the test.

At this time, there were only two elementary schools left in the area of Berlin in which the Tauchers were allowed to live that allowed attendance by Jewish children. They were Jewish schools by name only. Hitler had by now insisted that children of mixed marriages, "the privileged Jews", and Jews that had long ago converted to Christianity, many of whom did not even know they were considered Jewish, must attend the Jewish schools. This would turn out to cause all kinds of problems as these children had been raised in the violent mind-set of Nazism.

What Hank didn't divulge to Fred was what to expect. Fred's initial induction turned into a less than exciting experience. Classrooms averaged from one- to two hundred children, and the overall curriculum was ineffective, leaving most thirsty for more learning. Funding was curtailed, supplies were minimal, and there was an acute shortage of teachers. When lessons concluded for the day, the boys would gleefully run outside in hopes of playing for a while.

It turned out that many of the newest children, even the youngest, had already adopted the strong anti-Semitic beliefs of their elders, along with their brutal tactics: spitting, name-calling, beating, and kicking. These taunting attacks hurt, leaving the boys physically and emotionally bruised, with their minds dizzy and an awful swirling of nausea in their bellies. In the face of this scorn, Hank and Fred wanted to strike back in some form of defense. However, doing so was illegal and heightened the threat to their lives and their parents' lives. "Why could we not be accepted like other kids?" the boys lamented.

They were in desperate need of the tender care that only a mom could give them, and Therese would calm their nerves, reminding them that the problem was not that they were Jewish, but that other people were being taught to hate so much. Therese would thereafter walk with them to ensure that the boys avoided any trouble on the way home; undoubtedly, she was even more distraught than she let on over these hostilities and their effect on her sons' abilities to learn.

Although she did not possess a formal teaching certificate, she was very intelligent. Most afternoons she spent time teaching the boys, satisfying their thirst for knowledge with tutorials on the basics of reading, writing, and arithmetic. Finding each other's company much less stressful than the school environment, the boys enjoyed a favorite pastime after studies, playing checkers, which would lead to their later developing finesse in the art of chess.

On the first of September, 1939, the Nazis invaded Poland, bombing everything in sight and leaving its people without a country. This was the catalyst that finally prompted Great Britain's declaration of war against Germany, and thus, the official start of World War II. The Polish government, in a last attempt to win safety for the rest of its population, relinquished its entire Jewish population of more than 2 million to the Nazis, who soon locked them into ghettos. Many were simply left to starve.

In a railroad car outside of Warsaw, a German general presides over the official surrender of the Polish Army, September 28, 1939.

In a single ghetto in Poland, 40,000 Jews were walled in, with barbed wire everywhere, and under heavy guard. With no food, water, or sewerage they were simply left to waste away. And Hitler shocked his supporters when he extended the proverbial olive branch to Russia via the execution of a non-aggression treaty. With his hate of the Communists running almost as deep as his contempt of the Jews, eventually he would renege on this treaty, and Russia would soon be fighting the Germans.

WWII started on September 3, 1939, when Britain, France, Australia, and New Zealand declared war on Germany. Hitler had Italy and Austria on his side. The Allies would quickly include Canada, the USSR, and others. During the next few years, most countries in the world would be drawn into the conflict. Japan eventually sided with Germany; other countries would also join Germany, either through choice or by occupation. The USA did not officially enter the war until December 7, 1941, when Japan bombed Pearl Harbor. Then the United States officially joined the Allies, finally uniting with them against Nazi terrorism.

The dullness and austerity of the architecture in Berlin in those days was capable of leaving one cold and unimpressed. Permanently interwoven into the cityscape were the threads of the SS, who were customarily clad in black from helmet to boots. Their uniforms were adorned with bright red swastikas, which also draped the façades of buildings, and these representations of anti-Semitic dominance, whether on foot, in military vehicles, or on tanks, were on every corner.

Winter sun was exhausted in its tug of war, struggling to penetrate the clouds with its rays. The accumulated seasons of Nazi demoralization placed the Jews in the midst of endless mourning. Terrifying and dark listlessness took hold of the city. The vibrant creativity and glitter of an era was completely removed. Berlin, once the heart of many new cultural movements, was now without a heartbeat.

The Third Reich's intentions were becoming crystal clear as more was heard of the continuous mass roundups and confinement of Jews in Jewish ghettos and concentration camps throughout Germany and Europe. The world was finally listening and hearing the real truth.

Centuries earlier, self-established Jewish quarters, or stetls, always near the center of towns, became necessary to Jews' livelihoods. Most Jews did not own a vehicle, and this arrangement allowed them to interact with their Christian neighbors, participate in town hall meetings, work, and send their children to schools. Moreover, they were able to simultaneously continue with Jewish studies and traditions while in proximity to a synagogue and cemetery.

These areas were not designed by Jews to cut them off from Christian society, but rather to simplify their freedoms of life, personality, and culture. When Christian autocrats in Central Europe relegated Jewish people to live in ghettos, Germany showed itself to be predominant in this form of outright segregation, which was marked by the Jews' steady isolation. These stetls were not lacking in cleanness or comforts and always showed the pride of the Jewish people and their skills. Hitler would turn many of these areas into cruel ghettos of his most unwanted, walling them off and allowing few or no supplies to enter.

The sum of Jewish people in concentration camps and ghettos was far exceeding their holding capacity, so Hitler ordered mass executions. Inmates were marched at gunpoint to deserted areas, into the bitter cold and snow, and forced to dig large, deep trenches. Without blinking an eye, the Nazis forced the Jews to remove their clothing and line up along the edge of the pits only long enough to get gunned down. It was not uncommon for the Nazis to round up more than 10,000 Jews at a time in the cities of Europe and gun them all down.

In one town, the gentiles hauled the soccer bleachers out to the field for better viewing. One time, a lady gave birth right before she was gunned down. Sometimes, not all of the victims were dead before the bulldozers finished the job by guaranteeing that

Crematoria ovens at Buchenwald concentration camp.

all were covered over with the abundant earth. Another time, 2,000 Jews were forced into a pit after being stripped of their clothing, and Russian prisoners were ordered to bury them alive. When the Russians refused, the guards just killed them all, Russians and Jews. Hitler's goal was to kill millions of Jews and to do so he needed to kill in masses, not just a few hundred at a time.

Hitler, realizing his procedures were ineffectual in successfully killing off enough people fast enough, decided the time was ripe to equip most of the concentration camps with the mass extermination facilities and ovens. Rapidly, the camps in Poland were functioning mainly as facilities for murder *en masse*. The many thousands of Jews who were barely alive in ghettos and concentration camps across Europe and other places in the world under Nazi control were now being packed tightly into the cattle cars for their nonstop ride to oblivion.

Some Jews, such as those in Norway, were crammed onto ships destined for the European coast and then transported by rail to the death camps. The term melting pot would be apt, as many bodies would be made into soap. Millions of dollars of gold was yielded from the ovens, just by the recovery of the fillings of victims' teeth.

Chapter 10

Yellow Star rules are tightened, with harsher penalties and stricter enforcement; stars now must plainly say "Jude" on them.

Jews can't purchase milk or cigarettes.

Jews from other areas can't move into Berlin.

Most Jews in Berlin go underground. The term used to describe them when they briefly came out is "submarine."

Jews in France over the age of 6 must wear a star.

Students in Paris attack Nazis; many who do are arrested and sent to camps.

Germany invades the USSR; 2 million more Jews fall under Nazi rule.

The first reference to "The Final Solution" is made.

Use of gas chambers and mobile gas-wagons begins.

Pearl Harbor is attacked by Japan; America formally enters the war.

The Hitler Youth program was started in 1923, with 5,000 members in Munich. By the end of 1933 its membership had grown to 2,300,000. Much of this growth came when Hitler forced other organizations to merge with the Youth program. By WWII's end, it had about 9,000,000 members. In 1936, Hitler made it mandatory for boys and girls 10 years or older to join. The boys' program concentrated on physical and pre-military training, while the girls' program focused on preparing girls for homemaking, motherhood, and producing boys for the German Army's war machine.

Once enrolled, the youths could choose a specialty program, such as flying, motors and autos, weapons and protection, signals, medicine, or music. These programs would prepare the boys for duty in the German Merchant Marines, the Socialist Motorized Corps, military aviation, the Signal Corps, or other branches of service. The older boys received actual weapons training.

Once the youths reached age 19, they were drafted into the Reich Labor Service for one year. The RLS stressed physical work and iron discipline. After this, they were enlisted into the military. If they were of pure Aryan ancestry and showed leadership potential, they could join the SS instead of the regular army. The SS was immensely prestigious among the Nazis in Germany. Many would be recruited for the Death's Head troops of the SS, destined to be concentration camp guards.

The Youth program was also a military force from which manpower could be drawn if the need arose. Members were actively used in firefighting and assisted in recovery efforts that followed Allied bombing. They were also deployed in the Normandy invasion and the Battle of the Bulge and earned themselves a reputation for ferocity and fanaticism. During the Battle of Berlin, they were used as a last line of defense and were said to be some of the fiercest fighters. They were disbanded after the war as required by the Allies.

On September 1, 1941, the following decree, containing stricter requirements than had previously existed, was implemented: all Jews six years of age and older must wear a yellow Star of David with the word "Jude" sewn in the middle, and it must be securely attached to them. The star had to be worn in plain sight, which threatened Jews' safety outright. Jews had now lost their freedom to walk unencumbered down the streets or to go anywhere that was under Nazi control without being recognized.

Jewish women out walking next to a park, wearing yellow stars.

Immediately thereafter there was a drastic reduction of the hours during which Jews could be outside. Also, the purchase of food items was now only allowed between the evening hours of five and six o'clock, and then only at the few markets that were still open. By the time Jews were allowed to shop, there wasn't much left for them, unless they knew a sympathetic grocer who would save them some items at great risk to himself. Grocery items everywhere in Germany were very scarce, and most items were usually sold out by the time Jews were permitted to shop. Some store owners also chose just not to serve any Jews.

The Gestapo watched almost all grocery stores to ascertain that the rules were adhered to. Some store owners took advantage of the rules; they would double the price of grocery products during the hours when Jews could shop and so would make their largest profits during those times. Stores also did not stay open much after dark due to the heavy bombing that was now regularly occurring.

After recovering quickly from the initial humiliation, the Tauchers realized how being ordered to always wear the Magen David Star could put them at great risk by signaling to all that they were indeed Jewish. The star was no longer the declarative symbol of their faith that validated their courage and that served as a badge that solidified their principles. Now all it did was make them stand out as easy targets for abuse. Hank and Fred would experience, in each other's company as well as alone, severe trauma on numerous occasions throughout their childhood, due to having to wear the star. Harsh emotional scars may never disappear; neither does the sharpness of those painful memories fade. One can only hope for closure.

There was one particular event that Hank suffered alone. It was winter, 1941, and the glistening white of snow frost, from roofs and treetops all the way to the ground, made for a cold but beautiful sight. Hank was nine years old and believed that he was big and strong and that nothing could touch him. Hank wanted to go for a walk that day after school ended and to possibly meet up with a friend. In his youth and immaturity, he neglected to think of how fully having the yellow star on his outer clothing could hinder his safety.

A young boy, similar in age to Henry, wearing his yellow star. Sadly, this young boy was sent to Auschwitz the next year, where he died.

He headed to the Landwehr Kanal in the heart of Berlin, near the zoo, anxious to see the canal, wanting to stop at the water's edge that lay at the base of a slight incline. Hank walked down and stood there, composed, for what seemed like only a second or two. Yet he imagined Therese's concerns ringing in his ears. Letting common sense seep through, he turned to start away and get back home. Suddenly, his steps were halted; he was surrounded by two of Hitler's Youths, kids who had been trained to be thugs, who had seemingly sprung out of nowhere.

Blocking Hank's chance to flee, they violently tackled him, picked him up off the ground, and threw him so that he plunged into the icy waters. He could not swim; he had never learned how. Yelling, "Help! Help!" in panic, he tried to keep his head above the water, catching only the sound of their shrill laughter over his own screams. Feeling the numbing of his muscles, thrashing around in the frigid murky water, becoming weak, panting for breath, with algae and dirt filling his mouth, he was quickly drowning.

A gentleman passing by on his bicycle had witnessed the thugs' actions and, not hesitating, dashed into the canal to save him, even after recognizing the Jewish Star on Hank's jacket. Shivering and soaking wet, Hank could not believe it. He was overwhelmed by gratefulness to this heroic stranger for coming to his rescue. Being so shaken, Hank did not think to ask his rescuer his name. This compassionate fellow then went beyond his assumed responsibility and took Hank home, urgently, before they both froze.

The man paused at the apartment only long enough to dry off, purposely not wanting to risk more time there, leaving before Julius returned home. Julius recognized the tremendous risk this man had taken in getting Hank to dry land and home. Just entering this ghetto without a proper purpose was strictly forbidden to gentiles and was subject to severe punishment.

In his profound appreciation, Julius showed his gratitude with the offer of a custom-tailored suit. Therese had gotten the man's telephone number and gave the number to Mrs. Müller. A meeting was set up with a time for him to visit the laundry in the evening to arrange for measurements. It would require several visits for fittings at Mrs. Müller's laundry, where Julius was permitted to secretly use her sewing machine. Undaunted after having slaved away on the rail tracks all day, Julius, at his own risk, would work into the dead of night in the laundry to make the suit.

The two Hitler Youths, out of sheer mischief, had not hesitated to report the gentleman's actions to their commander, who had him placed under heavy Nazi surveillance. When the new suit was ready, the man came to receive the finished suit at the laundry, but upon his exiting the area, he was arrested and charged

on three counts: saving the life of a Jew; accepting Julius's gift, perceived as a bribe; and, the ultimate offense, soliciting a Jew for personal gain. By the law of the day, any gentile lending a hand to a Jew in any manner whatsoever faced the discriminative label "*Judenknechte,*" Jew Lover, and was guilty of a crime punishable by death.

Tenderhearted, Therese sought Gertrude's influence in hopes of helping to get this man released. Nothing was ever heard from this man; his kindness probably resulted in his death. The Tauchers could not understand why Julius was not similarly arrested. He was not even questioned. The family also was left wondering why Mrs. Müller's shop was permitted to remain open and why she too was not arrested. The Nazis knew all; the involvement of Julius and Mrs. Müller had certainly not escaped their all-intrusive eyes.

This would be the last year any schools in Nazi-controlled lands would be open to students. Hitler had finally closed all schools to all children, Jewish or not, without exceptions. Without another place where they could learn, Therese became the sole source of education for the boys. Although she had no formal teaching skills, she insisted that the boys continue their education daily. Using minimal supplies that she somehow procured, she refused to allow Hitler to deny her children an education.

Ravaged By Man, Not Nature: 1942–1943

Chapter 11

It was January, 1942. Muted reaction on the world stage opened the gates for the Third Reich's Final Solution; Adolf Hitler conferred with Heinrich Himmler and Reinhardt Heydrich, his top officials in charge of the arrangements. In Poland, Auschwitz-Birkenau, its sprawling acreage equipped with a host of murder factories, held the oppressive distinction of being the first site reserved for annihilation on an industrial scale.

Auschwitz held abominable notoriety for registering each of its prisoners selected for labor by means of a number tattooed on his or her arm. German doctors usually oversaw the arrival of new prisoners and were assisted by SS officers in the selection processing. If the new arrivals were strong and healthy, they were deemed fit for slave labor and sent to the right, where they each received their tattoo, regardless of whether they were men, women, or big strong-looking children, and then moved on. Auschwitz would turn out to be the number one camp for putting Jews to death.

Many men, women, and children would not qualify for labor and were sent to the left. Thousands each day would be marched straight to the ovens of hell. For the others, death was only a matter of a short, pain-filled time. Those not designated for immediate death received the dehumanizing branding and were then forced into abhorrent acts of slave labor, under the pretext of their lives' being spared.

A Jewish woman with three children walks toward the gas shower after the selection process.

Here also was Dr. Josef Mengele, the Angel of Death, performing experimental torture. Often his subjects were dying children, with twins being of special interest, who were brought to the camp laboratories in trucks on which was painted the Red Cross emblem and welcomed with a smile and an offer of candy. More often than not, women and children were put in right along with the unfit, infirm, and old.

Tens of thousands of people, their belongings set aside, waited, naked, having been told that they were just going to the showers and that their things would be returned to them when they came out. Instead, they were doused with the colorless, odorless hydrogen cyanide gas, their bodies were burned from their insides out, and their lives were expunged. Every day the putrid red ash belched from the chimneys of the crematories.

Easily manufactured, the Cyclone B stockpile was introduced first as part of the German Army's WWI arsenal, used against French troops. Recovered by the Allies at the end of WWII, it still contained enough crystals to kill an additional 20 million people.

In the autumn, the entire ghetto area where the Tauchers lived was forcibly emptied. Enduring recurrent upheavals, once again the family was expelled and sent yet deeper into a ghetto of Berlin, again just a few blocks away. The majority of their neighbors that were removed would be sent to the death facilities, their permanency certain. Bulldozers then flattened the buildings.

Their once fair city had become ravaged; any vestige of its former vibrancy was now reduced to dilapidated warrens. Moved to SW Solmstrasse 41, the Tauchers were amongst Jews, disabled Germans, and mixed families, all displaced and boxed together, enduring starving conditions. They were all awaiting their capture and transportation to a camp. Outside danger was always lurking, so only when hunger became unbearable did one go scampering out, looking for scraps, anything to soothe their hunger and thirst; somehow Therese always found something.

Now the days when Julius and Therese, with Hank and Fred in tow, would go about the town, innocent and alive, just enjoying the sights and family, were only memories. In these darkened days, stripped of everything, the reality was unmistakable: they were being hunted, and all were soon to be caught in a web, their mortality in the balance.

In sharp contrast to how he treated Jews, Hitler maintained a grand affection toward animals, an eccentricity in the scheme of his disregard for mere mortals. By ensuring the protection of zoos from demolition, he made a formidable statement to be sure, placing animals above the Jews.

Jews from all over Europe were being brought to Auschwitz: they came from France, Norway, Denmark, Czechoslovakia, Belgium, The Netherlands, Poland, Germany, Slovakia, Austria, Ukraine, Croatia, Romania, Greece, and other areas. Some arrived alive, while others arrived dead. The Germans would sometimes rig the transport trucks so that the exhaust would kill them on the journey. This would save time.

At Auschwitz, inmates (slave laborers) once were directed to dig up over 100,000 corpses that had been buried on the grounds in mass graves, and then take the bodies to be cremated in the new ovens. This was done to prevent possible groundwater contamination in the area.

Most Jews in Germany knew it was time to either go underground or die, especially in Berlin, where the Tauchers tried to maintain a semblance of living. With the Final Solution underway, the first railcars began leaving Berlin, taking the doomed to Auschwitz, sure of death, a thousand at a time.

The Nazis had all kinds of ploys to get their victims: announcing they had work permits or extra ration cards to hand out, needing people to show up at the square for a survey, telling people to stay home as "we have a new place for you to live and be sure to pack your things." Next thing they knew, individuals or whole families would be on their way to the camps, Auschwitz mostly, with all belongings stripped from them.

At this point, the Nazis considered a Jew to be unworthy of living. Age or sex did not matter anymore. The SS were even going into ghettos and just leveling them with bulldozers and snaring those who fled. Jews were crammed into boxcars, standing room only; lie down and you were dead. Many would fall, only to be stood upon by others, their wind cut off by accidental feet placed on their throats. No food, water, or services for days on end and no sanitation facilities except for a small, soon to be overflowing bucket.

Many Jews of Berlin did the only thing that they could do: they headed underground, sometimes alone, other times with their families. Jews' choices were few: they could either openly pretend they were gentiles or they could go into hiding. The problem with pretending was the ID issue. Necessary cards would include at least one or more of these: an ID card, residency permit, or work permit card. Other cards that might prove necessary would include ration cards, cards for clothing, cards for riding the trains, and even one to walk the streets. There were checkpoints everywhere, as well as roving patrols and the dreaded Catchers. Surprisingly, many chose to just wait to get sent off, especially the old.

In his drive to achieve a world *Judenfrei* (free of Jews), Hitler's fellow Nazi, Joseph Göbbels, turned to Catchers—Jews who turned in other Jews to the authorities. At first, many Jews would not believe that a Jew would turn another one in. But it was happening at a fast rate now, as so many Jews were getting desperate to survive and were turning to anything to survive just a little longer.

Anyone caught by the Nazis for any violation, small or large, was offered the false hope of release if they would turn in other Jews or their helpers. A Catcher worked for the Gestapo and was considered the ultimate turncoat. Two of the most notorious were Rolf Isaaksohn and Stella Foldflack, who often worked as a team. Stella was arrested after the war and served 10 years in prison; Rolf disappeared, although the rumors of a very unpleasant death have been heard.

One might find a place to rent but at an extremely steep price, as so many buildings had been damaged in the bombings. Hitler was more interested in weapon production than housing. Many rentals, regulated by new laws, required tenants to have their IDs checked before renting, especially if the properties being rented had been confiscated from the Jews. Rents were now 12 times higher than during the previous year; inflation was astronomically out of control.

Going underground meant the need for lots of money; rare also was the survivor who did not have an Aryan or gentile connection for help. Help was given by members of the Jewish Development Committee, the Norwegian Church, and various underground groups, among others, who helped the Jews as much as they could, often at the risk of death to themselves and their families.

Two Jewish teenagers, with false papers, living at a convent-operated old-age home.

Jewelry was commonly used in place of money, as it was an excellent store of value, easy to hide, and resistant to inflation. Hitler had by now made possession by Jews of any precious metals or stones illegal. Once people escaped the ghetto, it was as if they had escaped prison and become hunted convicts.

Going underground also could mean going homeless and just wandering around, or finding a place to rent to hide in, rarely going out: a room, apartment, house, a bombed-out building, a subway station, a shack, office, basement, garage, an orchard, or the back of a store. Many were helped by gentile friends or privileged Jews and sometimes by just plain strangers. Many Germans who did not believe in the Nazis helped out. Catholics also helped, many of whom believed that once Hitler finished with the Jews, they would be next. As the number of Jews left in Berlin dropped to fewer than 10,000, Jews were harder to find but were pursued that much harder.

Not having the traditional Jewish look was also a great asset, which really helped the Tauchers; also, the boys' young looks would become very important. The boys resembled Therese more than Julius, who had slightly more traditional Semitic features. Keeping clean with clothes tidy was also a challenge for the underground Jews, and not doing so would give them away. And if you were a male, why were you not at work? Some underground Jews took to using a crutch or a limp to hide their healthiness.

Most underground Jews had at least one gentile benefactor who would slip them some food or ration cards. The Berlin Jews also had to give up their penchant for obedience toward authority that they had developed during their lives; surprisingly many could not do this and died as a result.

The Wannsee conference in Berlin in January, 1942, was held to coordinate the efforts of various agencies in the Nazi government. One outcome of the conference was an effort to eliminate use of the words "killings," "extermination," or "liquidation," in discussion of the Final Solution. It was determined that the phrase "resettlement to the conquered lands," which really meant going to Poland and the gas ovens, would sound nicer and hide the harsh reality to the outside world. In late 1941 and early 1942, 25 trains left Berlin each day with 100 Jews per cattle car. After a while that number dropped down to fewer than 50 per car, as the Jews were becoming so scarce.

Chapter 12

The German Army is defeated at Stalingrad, USSR.

Women in Berlin stand up and resist terror in a six-day protest.

*The British Air Force pounds German targets, focusing on arms,
aviation, and ball bearing production.*

Jews are denied legal system protection.

Many Jewish ghettos in Eastern Europe are destroyed by the Nazis.

*Jews from Rome are sent to death camps in Germany,
with no response from the Vatican.*

Jews from Greece are sent to Auschwitz.

*All of Berlin's Jewish armaments workers are rounded up
for shipment to Auschwitz.*

An estimated 2,000,000 Jews are killed by the beginning of 1943.

*Hitler receives a gift of a dog to try to cheer him up after
the USSR defeat. The dog is named Blondie.*

The German mathematician D. Hubert, founder of modern math, dies.

*Allies start bombing Germany around the clock;
Germany bombs London in retaliation.*

Joseph Göbbels was fast approaching his goal of turning Berlin into a *Judenfrei* (Jew Free) area. To finally achieve his goal, he launched his Gestapo to raid the factories and round up all the privileged Jews left in Berlin, most of whom worked in the arms factories. They were Jews that had been deemed necessary for the war cause; most were married to gentiles. The Gestapo forcibly collected them, leaving, for the most part, their German spouses and mixed-ancestry children alone. These Jews were taken to a collection place at a downtown administration build-ing at Rosenstraße 2-4 and held for processing for their one-way trip to Auschwitz. Soon, their non-Jewish wives showed up bringing food, clothing, and blankets for their Jewish husbands inside. The crowd grew in the first few days to about 600 wives, who began shouting, "Let our husbands go."

The Nazis' extermination of the Jewish people had so far been kept behind doors closed to the German people at large, as well as to the world. Berlin was a very liberal city in Germany, having always had a dislike for the Nazis as a whole. The international news organizations were based in Berlin, so the Nazis were shy about their brutal acts being publicly known to the world. The Nazis also did not believe that women were capable of political action. They were caught in a dilemma, as they could not use force against these women without looking extremely hypocriti-cal. Soon, ordinary German citizens started joining the women, swelling the crowd to over a thousand, all taunting the Gestapo and the SS.

Finally, Göbbels saw he had no other choice than to release the men and to have 35 men who had already been sent to Auschwitz earlier that day returned. That day, about 1,700 men in Berlin and more throughout Europe were released, as the Nazis adopt-ed a hands-off policy toward *Mischlinge* (intermarried) Jews.

By January of 1943, Hank and Fred, now 11 and 10 respectively, had already known more suffering than an average person would see in a lifetime. What was occurring in their hateful world had become infused into all that Hank and Fred perceived, bring-ing real sadness into their eyes and depression into their hearts.

Looking at Julius, they were more and more concerned about his health, as his vigor appeared spent and his body gaunt from so many seasons of toiling. The enduring love his heart held for Therese and the boys had, for so long, been the sole source of his energy, feeding his return home each night after long days of slave labor and late hours at work.

That is until that fateful day of March 4, 1943. Rising with the dawn that morning, Hank was expecting Julius's embrace. Finding him not yet home, Hank went over to the curtained window, hiding in the shadows in hope of seeing him arrive. Julius had always made it back before. Suddenly, a lady came running up the street of the ghetto, past their place, shouting, "The Gestapo are rounding up all Jews and are tossing women, children, and babies into trucks like they were sacks of potatoes!"

Soon, the lady who owned the laundry outside of their ghetto where Therese occasionally worked came by, motioning Therese and Fred over to hear more closely. Not wanting to draw any attention to herself, she kept her voice low. She had come actually at the behest of Traute, whom she knew well, with tragic news about dearest Julius. Upon conclusion of the previous day's slaving, the Gestapo had set Julius aboard Transport No. 34, moving off along the tracks, bound for Auschwitz! How could this be? Therese was in agony, hearing those devastating words, wailing, "Not my Julius! Oh, God, No! Nazis, Swine!"

Helplessness coursed through Hank's and Fred's veins as they imagined Julius's final moments of freedom. The boys' bereavement at knowing Julius was probably gone from them forever was unconstrained. As the utter truth of this news set in, Therese was alerted further: the Nazis were on the way to their very own apartment building to arrest all.

Having seen the handwriting on the wall plenty of months earlier, Julius had sewn new clothes for the family, without the star—shirts, pants, and jackets—in the event of their needing to go into hiding at a moment's notice. Julius knew that a visible outline would show if the Star was simply torn off, a dead give-away, so leaving nothing to chance, God rest his soul, their father had prepared for the eventual situation.

In great haste, Hank and Fred put on the fresh clothing, stuffing into one small suitcase whatever other essentials they still possessed. Peeking out the window, Hank and Fred saw two Nazis, looking like Gestapo, who entered the main door and stormed up the stairs. In desperation, with everything happening so fast, Hank and Fred had to move quickly, out the rear of the building. Therese, clutching the suitcase, followed as the boys dashed into obscurity, on the run, their circumstances dire and knowing there could be no turning back now. Therese wanted to believe there were some good Germans still out there, willingly compassionate enough to administer protection. She must find help.

Once again, the only person who came to mind was Gertrude, the midwife who over the last decade had helped them abundantly. Was it possible that she would offer the family refuge at her own risk? Was there anyone she knew who might help? Sneaking through the city, it felt like ages before Hank, Fred, and Therese stopped to rest, once they were finally outside the ghetto. Far from safe, at least they were out.

Upon seeing a train station, Therese swiftly found a telephone and called Gertrude, who expressed happiness at their successful escape. And as Therese had hoped, Gertrude directed them to go to a train station in Berlin and then to travel to Spandau, a summer cabin area just outside Burgerablage. She insisted that they take three different routes to avoid detection, as the Nazis' eyes were everywhere. While traveling, Hank and Fred recalled their Julius and how wonderful he had been.

As promised, Gertrude was at the Spandau station to meet them. She told them she had a summer cabin nearby. They all proceeded to walk in the direction of her cabin, a good half an hour away. The reality of this woman's Nazi connections had certainly not slipped Therese's mind. Eventually, when Hank and Fred were walking on a wooded trail behind the two women, they saw Gertrude lean in close to speak with Therese. They caught their mother shuddering momentarily as she was informed of the situation. It quickly became apparent that this was not just any resort area, but was instead a retreat exclusively for Third Reich officers and their families, for vacationing between the spring and fall seasons.

Therese was shocked. She knew the family must go underground and hide somehow. She had never imagined that a mother of two boys would attempt what they now were going to do. She had never heard of anyone attempting such a charade.

Hard to swallow indeed, but what other choice did they have? Therese regained her composure and brought the boys into the fold as Gertrude issued firm instructions regarding how to respond in the event that they were asked anything personal about

Julius. Their answer was to be, "He's an officer in the German Wehrmacht (Army), serving in battle at the Eastern Front, and Gertrude, a family friend, has kindly invited us to stay with her and enjoy the warmth here, while getting away from the heavy bombings in Berlin."

The Aryan kids left each day for the city to attend a special school, which consisted mostly of Hitler Youth training courses. Naturally, it was necessary that Hank and Fred sidestep suspicion of their not being members of Hitler Youth. It was mandated that all youths 10 years and older attend. There would be exercises that would require showering afterward. Showering with the other boys was to be avoided at all costs, since as is customary for Jewish males, Hank and Fred had both been circumcised shortly after birth, and circumcision was not practiced among gentiles, especially in Germany.

At the same time, the boys had to make it appear as though they too were going to classes, knowing that any clue exposing their true identity would compromise their lives and surely cause misfortune to those others who had helped them avoid detection. They would clearly have to put on their best act to keep the strain of these circumstances checked. Gertrude left at the first opportunity and returned with a minimal number of items to help the family fit in, as at this moment everything they owned could be packed in one small suitcase.

Keeping secret a two-year lapse in their formal schooling, Hank and Fred left the cabin daily, dressed like the others, with books in their backpacks. Then they would slip away from the trail and into the wild woods. Under shelter of this canopy of trees and perennial underbrush, Hank and Fred felt some relief, their minds lulled by the breeze. They did not have the proper books, just some old books to fill space in their book bags. A matter of urgency did take up those few hours: gathering mushrooms, which were now their principal source of nutrition. Luckily, Hank and Fred were surrounded with abundant choices, and were able to avoid the poisonous ones while filling their satchels with many distinctly edible ones. The first hint of the kids returning from school would disturb their calm, and they would speed nervously back to the trail, merging in with the others. It was a routine that went on for days on end.

It was up to Therese to serve up these palatably inferior fungi. Hank and Fred knew how creative their mother could be, especially with the food supply running so thin. Her tasty concoctions did not disappoint, and every so often she added some other vegetable, a turnip perhaps, which emitted a pungent odor when cooked. Of course, at that point Hank and Fred were happy to have anything to eat.

Hank and Fred were truly each their brother's keeper, two lads who were never as strong alone as together, who had been forced into the greatest challenge of youth. Could the boys maintain anonymity and survive when so many others had not? Their bravado was an extraordinary feat; at some level they understood the necessity of combating their fright. Matured beyond their years and sworn to beat the odds, they focused solely on assuring their survival! Thankfully, Therese was bent on lending them her one-foot-in-front-of-the-other attitude, mindfully respecting the minutes and hours and days that followed; time was a gift never to be squandered, no matter how frail that gift was.

When the Tauchers received a postcard from Julius in Auschwitz, via Gertrude, on which he wrote, "I am well and will be home soon," Hank and Fred were stupefied. As quickly as the brothers had a hope of this being real, the hope vanished in the realization that the message was just part of another repulsive Nazi mind game that Julius had to comply with. They knew that one did not arrive at Auschwitz and live long. They knew that instead, within days of Julius's arrival at the Gate to Hell, he was gassed. The most precious husband and the best father that Hank and Fred could ask for was indelibly etched in their loving memories as a prince of a man.

Having little sense of what Gertrude's willingness to hide them actually meant, how long could the Tauchers expect to stay at a retreat where many of Hitler's political and social inner circle owned the small summer cabins? Therese, Hank, and Fred were frightened enough at the initial task of an incognito presentation and, amidst these surroundings, definitely unsure about taking such a risk for any extended period. Yet the days wore on as the family held it together.

Their deception was far from easy. The play of the other children was deeply rooted in the Nazi ideals. The other boys rarely mixed with the girls in play, as their future roles were already taking shape. The boys would be soldiers and the girls would become homemakers. The boys played mock war games and even hide and seek, where the one hiding would be a Jew, and a slip of the tongue, a misplaced Yiddish word, or a missed Nazi slang term could lead to Hank and Fred's being discovered. The boys and Therese also had to show respect to the constant stream of visitors that Gertrude received. Sometimes this would require standing with Nazis in full uniforms and having their photograph taken. More than once, they even had to celebrate a holiday and sing along while amongst Gertrude and Traute's peers.

In total, they pulled off their deception for five or six months. Had full disclosure of the impact of this serious game of pretend been given in advance, Hank and Fred might have bolted. In hindsight, they retained very few details and tremendous relief. Living on such a thin thread of hope, they hoped to never again have to experience such a dangerous balance of disguise.

The unheated cabins became particularly cold as fall approached. Families were now packing up and returning to their homes. By early October, the lakeshore area was like a ghost town, and Gertrude decided it was time for her to get back to Berlin. Once again displaced and on the run, needing some help in finding a safe place to stay, they were instructed by Gertrude to contact Traute, the deputized photographer for the SS.

Traute's newest directive, issued by the Nazis, was to photograph the corpses among the rubble of bombed-out buildings in order to positively identify these persons. Besides documenting the dead, her photos were now also being used as propaganda to inflame the German people's anger over the severity of the Allied bombing, in an attempt to stir the flames of their hatred. The Nazis used the pictures of dead people in twisted lies, for their own benefit.

Traute would always keep an eye out for a family of corpses that would match the Tauchers and could be used to help the family by providing IDs. It was no easy task for her to try to match a mother and two sons together. As extremely accurate records of the dead were kept by the Nazis, Hank and Fred had only a limited time to hold any IDs supplied by Traute before they would need replacing, an unavoidable inconvenience.

Upon finding a woman and two boys matching the Tauchers' descriptions, Traute had false documents drawn up, indicating that Hank and Fred both were a couple of years younger than they actually were, since the boys still did not look anything like their true ages. The family also received from Traute directions and introductions to a couple of places where they might be able to hide themselves for a short time, while waiting out their next move.

Red Clouds...Take Warning: 1944

Chapter 13

Conditions at Auschwitz become known to the public, due to escapees.

438,000 Hungarians and 500 Greek Jews are deported to Auschwitz.

40,000 Polish children are kidnapped for slave labor.

At the start of the year, the Jewish death toll reaches 3,000,000.

At least three known assassination attempts on Hitler occur.

In what is known as the Big Week, the US Air Force steps up its bombing in Germany, targeting aircraft production.

20,000 Gypsies are sent to Auschwitz.

400,000 Allied soldiers land on Normandy beaches.

Germany launches the first-ever missile in a battle, with only limited success.

Nazis raid a house in Amsterdam and arrest Anne Frank; she later dies, just before her camp is liberated.

Hitler orders Paris destroyed: "Turn it into a smoldering ruin."

Prisoners riot and blow up a crematorium and a gas chamber at Auschwitz.

Himmler orders the destruction of Auschwitz and Birkenau crematoriums in hopes of hiding what has really gone on there from the advancing Allies.

Fierce fighting continued throughout the world. The Allies were throwing everything they had available at the Nazi regime. The Allies successfully came ashore at the Normandy beaches, to try to wrestle back France and its neighbors from the Nazis, and then pointed east toward Germany and Poland.

The Soviets were also giving everything they had, from the north toward Germany. Most now felt it was only a matter of time before Hitler would fall. It couldn't be anytime soon enough for the Jews of Germany and Europe, most of whom were now in camps, with a few hiding underground, especially in Berlin. Many of those in Berlin came out only at night, to cheer the bombers on; everyone else was bunkered down in bomb shelters. They were the only witnesses to the battles above. They couldn't chance being discovered, so they avoided the shelters. The air raid shelters were key hunting grounds for the Nazis looking for Jews, deserters, and other perceived enemies among the gentiles. The streets and yards were empty; everyone else was in the shelters, especially the Nazis.

Gertrude Nölting was able to secure a job for Therese as a waitress at a hotel in Binz auf Rügen, a small resort town by the Baltic Sea, in the early part of 1944. With no other option, the family chanced a train route, armed with their newest IDs and passes, and arrived there without incident. Once again the Tauchers found themselves in the enemy's midst. Frequenting the hotel were Nazi officers in search of some rest and relaxation.

After their experience surviving undercover at Gertrude's summer cabin, Therese may have felt overconfident in their ability to hide in plain sight once again. But she was keeping her promise, doing what she must to secure their protection, not daring to consider how playing this close to the quick could get them caught. Presumably, in between this wicked crowd, the family would be safe—no one would suspect. Not once were their ID cards checked here. The Gestapo just could not fathom a Jewish mother and sons living in their midst.

It was a most terrifying experience for Therese, having to serve as waitress to these war-hardened Nazi officers. She had no choice but to wait on them with a smile and listen to their loud, boisterous talk. Fortunately, she did not show any classical outward Semitic traits. She had to work long hours among them, never showing her nervousness or contempt. She turned down numerous advances, always reminding those who approached her of her husband, who was away fighting for the homeland, and of her young sons, whom she had to see to immediately after work.

The family remained unsuspected at the resort for a few months, but as the gentile kids began to resume Youth schooling, Therese feared increased danger. Hank and Fred had to be enrolled in the nearby school, and after a time another student accidentally saw them in the shower, after physical exercise class, and noticed that they were different, circumcised. The young student was not sure what this meant, but in a very short time the truth would surely be revealed. Hastily packing for the umpteenth time, the family took the next train back to Berlin, where Allied bombs were dropping at a fierce rate, from the Americans' planes by night and the British by day.

Their identity cards needed replacing, as the Reich would surely soon be aware of the ruse by which the family had been using the identities of a deceased woman and two boys. Traute once again took care of this problem, securing them new papers. She seemed to keep the family's needs in her thoughts while she worked.

In approximately July of 1944, thanks to a lead from Traute, the family stayed with the Wüsthoff family, Germans whose politics were not aligned with the Nazi objectives of killing off the Jews and other minorities. Therese, Hank, and Fred were astonished at this family's willingness to lend them protection. There were still some good people trying to alleviate the Jews' despair.

The family's home in Erkner was a distance of an hour and a half by train from Berlin. Mr. Wüsthoff, a train driver, had a route that traveled the line from his home station to the terminus in Berlin, so with their false papers one of them could clear most patrol stops if the need arose to visit Gertrude and Traute's home. They only would go when absolutely necessary, as keeping a low profile was always a priority. Knowing Mr. Wüsthoff's arrival and departure schedule also helped; they tried to only ride his train, and he was able to allow one of them to sit in his compartment. Only one would go at a time, as the compartment was small and the Gestapo presence was always heavy on public transportation. Public transportation drivers in general did not like the Gestapo's constant checks as they caused frequent delays, resulting in scheduling problems.

No ID checks were usually made in Mr. Wüsthoff's small private area. What a trip! They lived with this family for five months, until the end of 1944; Mr. Wüsthoff was then drafted into the Wehrmacht (Army) and because of the obvious risk to his wife and children, it became impossible for the Tauchers to continue their stay. It had not been an easy time for all as one could not appear to be hiding, nor did they want to be seen. Just suspicion from a neighbor could lead to apocalyptical trouble. The Tauchers understood, and expressed tremendous thanks for all the Wüsthoffs had done, but again the family was left to search for other shelter, their options swiftly fading.

Subway and elevated train stations were one of the prime targets of the Allies during bombing raids, with many completely demolished. Some of these structures were still partially erect, skeletons, with their transports immobilized. Their underground passageways turned into sanctuaries that sheltered scores of people, all desperate for refuge from the Allied bombings.

The Tauchers, with no other options, turned to the shelter offered by a train station. Therese got them to the Anhalter Bahnhof. This train station would always also be their prearranged meeting place in the event that one became separated from the others.

Here they would hunker down, hiding from the bombs, while trying to blend into the crowd of thousands. The huge building above ground was no longer offering any shelter, having been reduced to a skeleton of bombed-out walls, with no roof. Everyone was seeking shelter underground, in the tunnels and platform areas. The Tauchers had found an empty kiosk, or booth, and this would be their spot.

The Nazis were always wandering around checking ID cards at all shelters. They had nothing better to do with the time on their hands, and were always hopeful in their quest of finding an unwanted amongst the wanted. It reached the point that those hiding were finding it extremely bothersome; many wished these brutal people would go away and leave them hiding in peace.

Therese thought it was best, when they did have to go out, to vary the routine. They would seldom go out as a group, and most times only one would go. She wanted to avoid the possibility, if they were stopped by the Gestapo, of the Nazis being able to use some of their favorite methods of interrogation, which she had seen or heard about. One favorite method was to separate detainees and compare their stories to find contradictions; another was to torture a family member while one was made to watch. There would always be the Nazis' false promises of rewards in exchange for cooperation with them. They were masters at interrogation and had no rules constraining their conduct.

Hitler had built huge bomb shelters in and near Berlin; some could hold up to 40,000 people and were fully supplied, built even to survive direct bomb hits and gas attacks. They were also heavily guarded by the Nazis, and ID checks were strict and regularly performed. Other official shelters were constructed in basements of large buildings; the interior walls were removed and the strong pillars were left to hold everything up. They too were fully supplied and manned.

Some people chose to dig holes in their backyards and cover them with wood, praying that they would not receive a direct hit of a bomb. Many did this to avoid the crowds at the shelters and the Nazis' presence. Other times, there were cases in which people just did not have enough time to get to a safer place. Most of the unwanted had no other choice but to seek shelter anywhere they could where they would be out of sight.

Attics in almost all of Berlin's buildings were emptied to reduce fire danger from bombing. The wide streets of Berlin also played an important role in minimizing the fire damage. The Allied pilots could not believe how Berlin refused to burn. Many underground train stations were turned into official bomb shelters and staffed by the Nazis. As the bombing intensified throughout Berlin, the necessity of shelter became increasingly important to survival; seeking shelter was no longer just a drill. Demand was high.

There was one particular young girl at the Bahnhof shelter who always stood out in the memories of the boys. She was as young as them, but their similarity ended there. She was playful and bubbly. She showed neither fright at the nearby bombs nor any concern about the situation. She always wanted to play or talk with the boys, but they would not have anything to do with her. After a few attempts, she gave up trying to make friends with them; the boys really were afraid of talking to anyone, let alone a girl of their same age. She had probably never been regularly in such close proximity to death as the boys had.

Therese, with brave practicality, never revealed a hint of her enormous internal tortures. In her passionate intent to protect the boys, she was inattentive to her own frailness, praying for strength and hoping that the next moment of seeing the boys would not be her last. Hearing the Allied bombs exploding around the clock, she knew the Nazis were getting a taste of their own medicine. From the hate they preached and the peril and murder they enabled, Hitler's puppets were being brought to their knees.

Grappling with the tragedy of their father's death and the reality of millions of Jews slaughtered, Hank and Fred struggled to suppress their panic, and appreciation for the value of their brotherhood was a shared sentiment. How much more could the family possibly bear? Their weary souls could not rest, always alert to the threat of being discovered.

Caught in the vortex of ever-present dangers, their only assurance of a substantial meal and a bath was at Gertrude's home. Walking or sometimes, in an absolutely unlawful act already forbidden to Jews for several years, gingerly sneaking onto a streetcar, one of them would visit her every few weeks. They chanced these meetings for more than just a hot meal and bath, as Gertrude often gave them ration cards and a bit of money. And when Traute received word of beefed-up dragnets, Gertrude made certain that whoever visited stayed overnight. This would cause terrible anxiety to the ones left waiting, but was unavoidable.

Maximum Storm Surge: 1945

Chapter 14

In January 1945, the Soviets liberate Auschwitz:
over 1 million had died there.

German fighter plane and tank production is reduced.

Romania and Hungry surrender and declare war on Germany.

Warsaw falls to the Soviets.

The Allied military, the Soviets, and the Red Cross liberate
many camps by the end of January.

The salt mines are discovered, stuffed with loot the Nazis had pilfered.

Jews are massacred by the fleeing SS.

American heavy bombers strike Dresden, leaving 135,000 dead.

Kurt Vonnegut will later write Slaughterhouse Five, based on
his experiences as a war prisoner in Dresden.

Peru, Chile, Syria, and Egypt declare war on Germany.

On March 18, a total of 1,600 US air bombers attack Berlin in one night.

On April 22, Sachsenhausen Concentration Camp
was liberated by the Soviet Troops.

The Allied forces were charging across Europe from the west to the east, while the Soviets were advancing from the northeast, both headed for Nazi Germany. Along the way, they began to discover concentration camps and evidence of mass murder and deaths. They encountered thousand of prisoners, most of them disease-riddled and starving, weakened from the demands of forced labor and years of maltreatment. The grim scene was not expected or planned for.

In late 1944, Soviet forces were the first to approach a major camp. They discovered Majdanek in Poland. Here they found evidence of mass murder and the gas chambers, along with graves filled with victims of genocide. The Nazis had fled and had tried to hide the evidence, but there was too much evidence and not enough time to successfully conceal it. Many other camps were quickly found, with many of them in varying stages of dismantlement, as there was beginning to be a shortage of Jews and other unwanted people to kill. The scope of the horrors became clearer as the forces continued fighting across Europe in 1945.

An abandoned train of boxcars, found by the Allies, that was returning to Germany from Auschwitz; personal effects of Auschwitz victims are scattered on the snow-covered ground.

In early 1945, the Soviets liberated Auschwitz, by far the largest concentration camp and extermination center ever built. Over 1,000,000 had perished there. Large piles of dead and unburied were found in the numerous camps. Thousands of emaciated prisoners were found barely still alive, many of whom died in the days and weeks to come due to their weakened condition and poor health. Only after the discovery of these numerous camps did the scope of the Nazi terror and of the unspeakable conditions and acts that had existed become clear to the world.

The Allies dropped 3,000 tons of bombs on Berlin on February 3, and again on February 26, to soften it up for the Battle of Berlin. On March 18, a total of 1,600 US bombers attacked Berlin. The Soviets were the first Allied ground troops to arrive near Berlin in March, 1945. Just outside of town, in the Seelow Heights, they were held back repeatedly by the Germans, who had the advantage of being dug deep into the hills. After days of heavy fighting, in which tremendous losses were absorbed, costly advancement

An American tank crashes through a barbed wire enclosure holding Allied POWs imprisoned in a camp west of Berlin, April 8, 1945.

was finally achieved by the strong Soviet forces. This was the scene of some of the heaviest and hardest fighting seen in the war, with huge losses of lives and equipment on both sides.

The Soviets regrouped for two weeks, resting and refreshing supplies. At that point, the Nazis had to face the reality of possibly losing the war. Their supplies were lacking and they were literally out of fuel. Troops were pulled from other front lines to fight in the last stand to save Berlin from falling. Many German citizens had by now become disgusted with the Nazis' seeming demise and the enormous amount of land laid to waste by the fighting. Rumors were also swirling around about the harsh conduct of the advancing Russian Army toward the German citizens they encountered.

The date was March 1945. It would turn out to be only four weeks before the end of the war. This was Fred's day to visit Gertrude Nölting. He approached a streetcar at a crowded station, boarded, and had to stand. Before he could do anything, Fred spotted what he assumed was a Gestapo officer aboard who was checking ID cards. Was this his judgment day? Steadying himself, while praying for invisibility, Fred could only stand there. Hitler's regime had hit its eleventh hour, but its pursuit of Jews was only heightened during its final chance to wipe them out. Publicly effaced for 12 years, the Jews were now considered outlaws, their very existence illegal.

The officer ordered the driver of the streetcar to keep it still while he stomped down the aisle of the trolley checking everyone's IDs. When he saw Fred's ID, he suddenly halted. Being a very young-looking 12 year old, whose voice had not even changed yet, Fred had no reason to believe that his newest ID card would not pass.

But what Fred had neglected to recognize was that his age on the ID was 11. The first recruitment age for Hitler's Youth was 10, and he needed to be in the Hitler Youth uniform as required in public for a child of his age.

The officer made his demand as he glared piercingly into Fred's eyes: "Let me see your Hitler Youth ID!" This question confused Fred, as he had not reckoned on needing this card. His mouth was so dry he could barely speak. The officer barked, "Why aren't you in the proper uniform?" Trying to quell his shaking, his heart feeling as if it was about to fall out of his body, Fred answered, "My uniform is being washed and I forgot this ID." But the officer refused this story. Fred heard him call out to another officer to come onto the streetcar.

Fred will never forget how they looked at him. Everyone on the streetcar was looking at him, their expressions full of repugnance. "Drop your pants," the Nazis ordered. He was stupefied, feeling separate from his body. How could they violate him, just a kid, like this! Truly persecuted, he would be taken away for certain now; his Judaism was revealed, naked and debased. Women remarked that they had never seen a Jew's penis before. Fred was sure he was going to die. After dragging him from the streetcar by the scruff of his neck, the Nazis flung Fred to the curb, jabbing their shoes into him. One boy even went as far as to urinate on to Fred. All the while he heard the deafening cheers and clapping of onlookers. "Great, another Jew Pig found and arrested!" some screamed.

The two Nazis yelled over the ruckus, "We are not going to hurt you; we only want to ask you some questions back at our headquarters." Fred, who was much smarter than his years told, saw past their feeble promise. Virulently gloating, devoid of contrition, Hitler's brutal players were just winding up. Picked from the curb, Fred was thrown onto the back of their truck. He thought about Therese and Hank, who would be waiting for his return; he felt feverish, and his body trembled uncontrollably. He had to force his turbulent mind to attention. "How in God's name can I survive this?"

The Gestapo held Fred captive at their compound for almost two whole days, during which he was interrogated while being terrorized. They asked the same questions over and over. Where was he living? Who had been helping him? They were dying to know, but Fred vehemently denied them answers, daring only to give them his name as on his ID card. He was taken to the Gestapo headquarters and prison. Fred was interrogated again, and suddenly they were beating him, their blows so powerful he fell into unconsciousness.

When he came to, his movements revived their attacks, again and again. Time after time doom fell upon him, but his will was not weakened, and in his head he devised a plan. If he pretended to be unconscious, he might save his life. Thus, he feigned passing out, which caused them to leave the room. Fred in quiet fury silently cried, "WHEN WILL THIS PAIN STOP?"

For a short time his ruse worked, but before long the officers were back, their cruelty only intensified, and they cast Fred several times into a tub of ice water and then immediately into another, scalding hot. When this water treatment did not get the desired results they switched to other methods of coercion. This went on for a long time, yet their attempts to torture him into submission failed. Just a boy, he had withstood their intimidation, crushing their power. Eventually, they were able to get his real name, but nothing else. He would accept death rather than divulge the whereabouts of his mother and his brother, claiming they had been lost. Nor would he reveal the kind ladies or the good Germans who had helped them so much.

Toward the end of the second day, Fred was placed on a train headed for a camp. In the steaming, crammed cattle car were many Jews, gentiles arrested for keeping Jews, children (many already lying dead), and Soviet prisoners of war. This cage was a death trap. Fred had never been so terrified as at that very instant; all the other frightening times of his short life could not compare. Crawling along the German countryside, the train, as if pushed only by a dragonfly's breath, rolled for what seemed like days. Speed was kept at a minimum to avoid detection of their traverse, while securing a growing accumulation of bodies. The air was choked by the putrefaction.

Fred saw the dread coming over the faces of human beings who were scarcely alive, withering from starvation and mental infirmity, their bowels uncontrollable. His own body was so weak that he was near collapse, fearful that he could not stand for another minute. He could hear the screams and pleas from those who had fallen and were being stood upon by those still standing. Sadly no one could do anything to help. Many of those standing were not even conscious, and were only being held upright by their situations. At 12 years old, amidst this horrid reality, his soul in agony, with no escape, Fred was now ready to die.

"Let me just lie down and die," Fred agonized. "Now! Before the Nazis' bullets send me to my grave or I'm sent to an oven. Why let the pains continue in this hopeless situation?" Harrowing thoughts of Julius flooded in, brought to mind by all that had been inflicted upon him in these last few distressful days. Julius had not relinquished his strength, or his courage, Fred reminded himself. Fred seemed to sense the presence of his father, once alive but no more. In his head Fred heard Julius's voice telling him that he must follow his example. "You cannot give up!" What about Therese and Hank? How could he add to their anguish?

One of the Soviet POWs he was pressed against adamantly expressed to him, in Yiddish, "To stay alive you must remain upright! We will soon be at the Dachau Camp." Tending to Fred, the Russian soldiers would not allow him to succumb to the seemingly never-ending days and nights in transit. They assured Fred that they would help him get through, and they did keep him up. The train crawled to a slow stop, there was no sensation or jolt of stopping, and it just slowly dawned on the ones that were conscious that the train had reached its destination. Fred, along with hundreds of others, had arrived, just yards from the outside of a camp: Sachsenhausen.

Everyone on board assumed that the camp was Dachau. Everyone's dream of a full life was, apparently, about to be terminated. There was no sign welcoming them to Sachsenhausen, only the stench of death. Typhus was epidemic at this time at this camp; it was common throughout most camps toward the end of the war. Very little could be seen by those still alive in the boxcars. Barely any light was allowed through the wooden slats and none could penetrate the mass of bodies. None knew for sure how many days or nights they had been in the cattle car, nor did anyone know how many miles the train had traveled or in which direction.

Sachsenhausen was just outside the northern edge of Berlin, near the town of Oranienburg. Since 1936, this concentration camp had mainly been a place where political prisoners and POWs were sent; several hundred thousand Soviet soldiers had died there, many while undergoing brutal treatment and medical experimentations. The camp was also a favorite place for holding the Jehovah's Witness prisoners. Records would show later that approximately 3,000 Catholic priests and bishops who preached against the Nazi conduct, no matter how minutely, had also been sent to Sachsenhausen during Hitler's regime.

Fred anticipated the tearing open of the doors and the breathing of fresh air, while knowing it was only a matter of time before his death. But another day would slowly pass, only witnessed through slats in the cattle car boards. The Nazis could be seen marching endless groups of helpless prisoners out of the camp and into the woods. Then rounds of gunfire followed, and only the trigger-happy Nazis returned. Then more inmates would be marched out, followed again by gunfire, and the same routine was repeated over and over. The Nazis were doing their final, grim housekeeping chores.

The Soviet Army had begun to move from the Seelow Heights, on its final push to Berlin, and was now approaching Oranienburg, possibly not even aware that the camp existed. "Stalin's Organs," the Soviet artillery cannons, were spitting out a whistling and shrieking barrage of artillery shells, announcing their steady advancement. Never before had such guns dished out such heavy punishment. Over a million rounds poured from the Soviets' cannons over the next few days.

Finally, late one afternoon, Fred's mind was alerted to the sounds of air raids, heavy bombing, and artillery fire. For the annals, the date was April 19, 1945; the Allied war machines were leveling the Nazi murder houses. Somehow the cattle car door got unlatched from the outside, opening upon a confused scene. No one knew where they were, but everyone seemed to have the same thought: Run!

Fred thought he might muster enough strength to jump off the train, but a Soviet soldier, realizing Fred would most likely kill himself in doing so, swept him up and lifted him into the arms of another Soviet prisoner already on the ground. Then they ran, escaping in the direction opposite to that where the SS and armed camp guards seemed to be, racing across a highway and into the woods. All around them, artillery explosions shook the ground and the shrieking sound of incoming rounds perforated the sky.

Self-preservation being the main objective, the soldiers would fight to the end. A life for a life is not a credo of Judaism, yet in war it must be. The Soviet escapees went seeking shelter in the forest, where they spotted Hitler Youths being trained by older comrades in the art of firing rifles. The Soviets, having no weapons of their own, quietly took positions. After sneaking up from behind, they finally rushed forward and began disarming the Nazis, losing a few of their own in the scuffle but killing all of the Nazis, old and young.

Moving just a few yards away, they began searching for food and water. Finding both just a few meters away at the Youth campsite, they gave Fred just a small amount of food—only a little at a time, to prevent him from getting sick—and a bit of water to wash it down. Then they finally took a little rest, stretching cramped limbs while trying to remove some of the filth and stench that clung to their bodies.

Finally, with darkness giving them some shelter, the Soviet soldiers returned their attention to the dead that lay about. Fred watched them slip into the Nazi uniforms that they had stripped off the dead and re-dress the dead in their Soviet garb in hope of hiding their ruse, and then, without words, they simply disappeared. Half out of his mind, Fred was left to fend alone, wondering, "How could they have simply deserted me?" He had thought they cared. They had agreed amongst them that Fred was much too young to help in fighting and could possibly slow them down.

Now isolated in the chilled blackness and surrounded by the group whose liquidation he had witnessed, Fred was overcome by extreme sadness and worries. Finally, all he could summon was a cry of agony over the recent days of horror and suffering. The vividness of this trauma would never leave him. Finally getting control of himself, he knew he had no alternative but to do what the soldiers had done.

Removing the Hitler Youth uniform from a boy's lifeless body, young Fred shivered as he put the uniform on his own body. He headed to the main highway, which he had crossed what seemed like an eternity ago, while on the train. In the moonless night, Fred saw lights from a car fast approaching and started waving crazily. In utter shock, Fred realized it was a German military car that was stopping.

Two SS officers jumped out and demanded to know what he was doing on the road at this late hour. Clothed in the Hitler Youth uniform, Fred told them he was in the woods with a group being trained to shoot "when our enemies attacked, and being unarmed I pretended to be dead. I was the only one who was not killed." "Hop in, we are going to Berlin," the Nazis told him. Those words were music to Fred's ears. He must get back to Therese and Hank.

What do I say if they ask me what unit I am in? What is my name? Fred worried; he hadn't bothered to look at the dead boy's ID. His worry soon quieted, for the Nazis were more concerned with their own survival than with questioning their young passenger. Fred no longer believed that the Nazis were a threat to his existence. There was no mistaking he was still very much alive, and these fiendish Nazis were now on the edge of defeat. "Their day of reckoning has now come," he bravely thought to himself.

When the officers stopped at their destination, Fred got out and walked away, surviving what had seemed to be his inevitable doom. He now set off in hopes of finding Hank and Therese at their long-standing, preset meeting point, in case of separation: the Anhalter Bahnhof. Fred was not prepared for the sight that awaited him there.

Chapter 15

Soviets pour 1 million artillery rounds into Berlin.

On April 24th, Soviet troops enter Berlin.

Adolf Hitler gets married in April to Eva Braun; both commit suicide on April 30, in his Berlin bunker, at which time Hitler's dog Blondie also dies.

On May 2, the Soviet Army accepts Berlin's surrender.

Looting and rape is widespread.

On May 7, 1945, the Unconditional Surrender of all German forces to the Allies is signed.

Peace falls over Europe.

Joseph Göbbels commits suicide along with his wife and eight children.

General George Patton dies at age 60 from injuries in a car crash.

Now back in Berlin, Fred returned to the train station, which had received extremely heavy damage from the new bombing attacks from the Allies' planes. The destruction was beyond description. He was trying to find a way through the rubble to enter the underground portion where Hank and Therese should be waiting. In shocked surprise, Fred caught sight of his mother, who happened to be out just then getting a small container of water from a fire hydrant. He ran to her.

She was overjoyed at seeing Fred; her loving eyes searched him for assurance that he was all right, and she wrapped him tightly in her arms. After the initial shock of seeing Fred alive and wearing an actual Nazi Youth uniform, she quickly led him into the underground area, and they found Hank. Therese pulled a change of clothing for Fred from her small satchel, lest he be summoned to duty by the numerous Nazis milling about.

As much as he wanted to release all of the treachery he had suffered, he realized the need to hold back, to shield her from the furtherance of undue distress. His mother did not have to hear every detail. She had been frantic when Fred disappeared, and what she must have imagined was probably as bad, if not worse, than what he could have shared of his dark journey.

The miracle was that he had survived and that the family was now back together. Their best strategy would be to stay off the street and hide from the bombs until the war was finally over. Therese vowed that from then on they would never be divided up, believing their unity made them more capable of getting out of this hell alive.

Berlin was now aflame. Soviet troops were fighting to occupy the city, freeing the innocent and taking the murderous Nazis prisoner. For days the fighting went on. It was an ugly scene in the streets as the final fighting between Hitler's forces and Soviet soldiers took place. Body parts were everywhere: arms, legs, heads, and torsos without heads. Hungry people were out butchering dead horses that had been used to move military supplies, desperate in hunger for anything edible.

The SS was being kept busy shooting at the enemy, deserters, and anyone without papers. Bombs dropping, artillery fire, tanks blasting, and heavy and light gunfire seemed to be everywhere. Sometimes a building would be the only thing separating the forces, and sometimes just a wall. Terror and confusion ruled the city streets. This went on for block after block.

In the major cities of Germany, food was extremely scarce. Even the bomb shelters had bare shelves. In the countryside, small farms still had supplies, but there was no way to get them to the population in the cities. Fuel was scarce or nonexistent, and troops from each side would regularly confiscate commodities if their rations were exhausted. Traveling was not safe due to the fighting, and the few trains able to operate offered only limited service. There were no trains leaving the central area of Berlin. Only the brave or desperate would attempt the dangerous journey out of the city in search of food.

In the days that followed, Therese selflessly tackled the chore of finding food and water for the family, slipping into the bloodied streets only when the famine in their bellies became too severe to bear. The most readily available commodity was death and chaos; fighting ruled the city. Making it to the end of the war was everyone's goal.

Finally, on May 2, the Reich Chancellery surrendered the city of Berlin to Marshall Zhukov of the Soviet Army. The document was signed by General Weidling, commander of German troops in Berlin. This was far from the end of the fighting here or elsewhere, where fighting officially continued. In Berlin, things might have actually gotten worse, although the Allies did halt their bombing of the city. In many areas the fighting just continued as if nothing had happened. In most areas, mass confusion ruled. The Nazis' POWs and slave laborers were set loose. A common ruse involved Nazis putting on Soviet uniforms, while others put on civilian clothing, some complete with a Jewish star. Everywhere, false Jews emerged among the few who had actually survived.

The Chancellery building in Berlin was where the Reichstag convened and had offices. Deep underneath, Hitler had constructed a two-story, thick-walled, cement and steel bunker. It had over 30 rooms for offices and living areas. This was where, just a few days before Berlin's fall, Hitler, his wife Eva, and Joseph Göbbels and his family committed suicide, along with a few other important Nazis. Only moments before his suicide, Hitler ordered his troops to fight to the end. He also left instructions, along with ample gasoline, to have the bodies burned in order to prevent the possibility of his dead body being publicly displayed. The dog Blondie was also among the dead.

Since 1941, Nazi forces had laid to waste numerous tracts of land and cities in Russia. More than 20 million Russian military and civilians were dead. There were fears of retaliation, and the masses of both sides were close to starvation. The "Big City" had finally fallen. It was no longer the political, economic, and communication center and power base of the Nazis' Reich.

Now the Soviet soldiers went on a looting and rape rampage, fueled by the liquor they found and the suffering they had endured in securing their prize. It would take a few days before most Berliners were even aware that the German Army in Berlin actually had surrendered. Unexploded bombs erupted, set off by the numerous fires throughout Berlin, and scattered gunshots rang out for unknown reasons. German tanks sat quiet, out of gas, while many Nazi soldiers stood next to their now quiet guns, hands raised, finally out of bullets.

In the distance, fighting could be heard, which continued for a few more days, just outside the city. Screams constantly arose from the wounded that were dying in the streets. Women were being raped, while other men and women were being rounded up and marched off as prisoners. Confusion and grief ruled the streets; most, wisely, just stayed hidden, wondering, "What is going on?"

At this point, the water in the tunnels was considered unsafe to drink due to the numerous broken water and sewage pipes. Most of the city's sewage, water, and electrical systems had been laid parallel to the tracks during the original construction. The underground pump stations sat idle, as electricity from above ground had been ruined by the bombings. The little light there was came from a few candles or lamps; it was hot, as the ventilation systems were also not functioning. The Nazi command posts had the only generators and only a little gasoline. It was a scary, hot, and dark place to be.

"I'll be right back," Therese comforted, leaving the boys just briefly to fetch water from the only remaining known fire hydrant that was working near the tunnel. It was the fourth day of May, 1945, just three days prior to the war's official end. Everyone knew the end was near for the Nazis. And it was on that day that the boys would see their mother for the last time. Like a flash of light, their mother, with her sweet hugs, the sparkle in her eyes, and the pride she held for her two greatest achievements, was gone. Never would Hank and Fred look upon her beautiful face again. The boys' unbridled emotions surfaced; they were weeping and in pain. Had the Nazis seized her?

While the boys waited, they tried to stay optimistic, their eyes roaming the very confused scene. They were surrounded by ordinary Germans, many wounded, many sick, with deserters from each side, wounded Nazis and healthy ones. There were also a large number of Nazi command and defensive forces hidden behind sandbag command posts, ready to fight to their end. Many wondered if the remaining gasoline might be used to seal the fate of them all, in a cowardly final act by the Nazis.

Suddenly, the crowd started to push deeper into the station tunnels. The boys continued to resist, but to no avail, and they were pushed from their kiosk. The tunnels were slowly being filled with water and sewage, and the Nazis still controlled the main entrances and were intent on letting no one in or out. All kinds of rumors were being passed along, mostly about who was trying to kill whom. The crowd remained intent on going deeper and possibly attaining survival at the other end of the long tunnels.

The water stank, and people shouted to not drink it, warning that it would make anyone who did very sick. Finally, after a few hours, the boys emerged on the streets of Berlin, quite a few blocks from the station. Once they figured out where they were, they began the dangerous trek back on the unruly streets. It was a dangerous game of hide and seek, in which no one had any idea who was the devil. In total darkness, they found their way back to the station's ruined main entrance and waited for their lost mother.

In the course of the Soviets' swift offensive, maybe she was among the many civilians who were taken prisoner; the grim reality was that so many of the women were raped. Perhaps she simply became too weak, near to dying, and waited in some quiet corner for death to come. As their conjecturing was leading them nowhere, they opted to stop their ruminations. While the truth seemed unfathomable, they reflected on what they felt sure of: Therese's love of her boys and her willingness, always, to give her life in an instant to save theirs. In the turmoil of warfare over the course of those final days, no real logical conclusion took shape. They chose to believe that most likely Therese was killed in crossfire.

The Soviet soldiers knew the German Army was the enemy, but what about the citizens? They had no way of knowing who the good Germans were or which were bad. One large problem was the language barrier. This dilemma would take some time to work out; in the meantime, all were, necessarily, treated with skeptical caution. Very few Russian soldiers spoke German, and even fewer were ones who spoke Yiddish. The few who did found themselves quickly brought forward to help, and many of these men were promoted in rank, sometimes right on the spot.

In Berlin, 5,000,000 were homeless, and all were shell-shocked, none more so than the underground Jews of Berlin. The underground Jews, their numbers estimated from as few as 200 up to only a little more than a thousand, started to emerge. They tried with little luck to communicate with the Russian-speaking Soviets. The soldiers also found it hard to believe that there were really any Jews that had survived the mayhem. For many of these Jews, it was the first time they had seen daylight in years.

On May 7, 1945, at his headquarters in Reims, France, the Supreme Commander of the Allied Forces in Europe, General Dwight D. Eisenhower, accepted the unconditional German surrender. It was signed in person by General Alfred Jodl, chief of the operational staff in the German High Command. The guns were finally silent; the piecemeal surrenders of the German Army that had been happening across the world over the last few days were now formally finalized.

There was one exception: the Soviets who were occupying Berlin required that Germany sign a separate unconditional surrender document with them. At the newly established Soviet headquarters in Berlin, German Field Marshall Wilhelm Keital signed this additional document on May 9. One might wonder if this wasn't the first sign of the upcoming long, cold war.

The first thing many people noticed at the end was the quietness that settled over Berlin. A few dared to look out, then suddenly people appeared and shouting was heard in the streets: "The war

Soviet soldier looking at a map of Berlin on May 7, 1945, while in the heart of the city.

is over, the Third Reich is toppled." "THE WAR IS OVER!" "No more killing, is it true?" "Oh, dear God, it's finally over."

Peace at last. Hank and Fred had survived the unimaginable and stepped out at last from where they had hidden and into the blinding sunlight. Bodies were everywhere, and they bemoaned the grisly sights, hoping to find their beloved mother amidst this hideous scene, but she was nowhere. Turning to each other, now orphaned, they wondered: what were they going to do? Could they expect Gertrude and Traute to take care of them? Surely the women would be saddened at the news of their mother's death. Were they even alive?

Fred and Hank did not attempt to go to Gertrude's home immediately at the end of the war. Stubbornly, they felt it was best to wait for a while, in case of their mother's return, however unlikely, and to allow some time for peace to settle in. Rather, they befriended a small group of Soviet soldiers who had built a small fire on the street across from the ruins of Anhalter Bahnhof. The boys soon found themselves at work. With their knowledge of the inner city and the fact that they had been the oppressed, not the oppressors, they became the soldiers' guides to getting around Berlin. The Soviets maps were of little use to them as Hitler had changed the downtown street names during his reign of power.

For the short term they felt safe, and the soldiers gave them food and water. Were Gertrude and Traute still alive? Was their home still there? The boys wondered. Berlin seemed to be totally destroyed. "If we can't find them, let's see if Mrs. Müller has survived."

Following the Soviets' initial occupation of Berlin, the city was divided into four sections: Russian, American, British, and French.

It was not until a few days following this division that Hank and Fred made the attempt to go to Gertrude and Traute's home. Walking in that direction, the boys believed they would be welcomed with open arms; the women always had cared for them.

No human beings, children notably, should ever be subjected to violent oppression, for they will forever move through life permanently altered by what they have seen and felt. Yet there is no question that many children possess a remarkable resilience and courageously pledge that their lives will not be ruled by adversity but will be allowed to soar, evincing positive understanding and a purposeful direction. History can make or break people, with the restoration of a normal life the greatest miracle.

Approaching the building where Gertrude lived, on the heels of their emotional collapse, Fred and Hank thought that it had, possibly, been destroyed in the raids, but it appeared intact, and they felt their worries lighten. She just had to be there. Opening the door, she looked down at their haggard figures, her expression a mix of shock and concern, and then fondly embraced them in one big hug.

Escaping the boys was a full understanding of how necessary Gertrude had become in their lives. The strong bonds resulting from her exceptional friendship with Therese had sprung 12 years earlier. As inconceivable as it was, apparently Gertrude initially had no clue of her friend Hitler's intent to eradicate the Jews. She had by now destroyed any evidence that would or could connect her to him.

They understood her grandmotherly attachment toward them, yet her warmth exacerbated their yearning for their dear mother.

In the midst of this state of hollowed despair, all Fred and Hank could think about was each other's pain. Would they ever come to terms with the deaths of not one but of both of their parents? They had no knowledge of any surviving family member, however remote the relationship may be, or for that matter of any friends. In sum, it just was too much to take in. The boys talked like adults about all that they had endured, but it all was really hard to understand.

The boys felt their well-being was best served by not wallowing in grief; their parents would never want that from them. Yet they were alone at 13 and 12. In truth their world was destroyed, and they were in no condition to seriously contemplate any sort of undertaking. Nevertheless, strangely, they had a sense of readiness for their independence and anticipation about stepping into the Great Unknown, where only their dreams had gone.

Gertrude and Traute did offer them their home, and the lads, considering their past circumstances, were indeed made exceedingly comfortable. With all that the boys had weathered, Gertrude was very sympathetic to Hank and Fred's needs for solace, a period of adjustment, and healing. Finally, Hank and Fred did not need to run anymore.

The four of them living together was like nothing the boys had ever experienced, for Gertrude and Traute were wealthy and spared no expense, trying their best to be surrogates for all that the boys were wanting. Hank and Fred were reminded of the simple joys of a lost childhood—freshly baked cookies and other favorite sweets, quiet walks without the need to worry—and slowly the ability to laugh aloud returned.

Some of the Soviet soldiers, who Fred and Hank had amazed by their very existence, a result of somehow surviving all those years in Berlin as Jews, had become friends. And because of Fred and Hank's help in getting them around in the city, they had procured for the boys, from the Soviets' Berlin HQs, written documents which allowed them free, safe travel around Berlin.

With this new-found freedom, the boys eventually went in search of an American army installation they had heard about, known to be near to Gertrude's home. They also tried at this time to find Mrs. Müller. The area where her shop had been and nearby, where the Tauchers had once lived, had received a lot of heavy bombing and many fires were still smoldering. Numerous unexploded bombs were also lying around, adding danger. The area was really unrecognizable to the boys; they fled from the grim scene, vowing to return at a later date. Only a fraction of their synagogue was still standing. They could only guess where Mrs. Müller's shop might have once been.

Finally at the US Army installation, they found the entrance and a guard manning the gate. Now they had a problem. The guard did not know German, nor did the boys speak English. The boys believed that someone on the base must surely know some German, but inflections and exaggerated hand gestures were getting everyone nowhere. Firmly standing their ground, the boys were willing to wait until someone came along who could help them.

It just so happened that after a short time, an American army truck came along, and the one soldier in it overheard the confused situation. He put on a big smile and asked the boys *"Sind wir Jüdisch?"* Are we Jewish? After so many years of fear of their identity being known, the boys hesitated before realizing that the Americans were really the good guys. They admitted that they were Jewish and that their father had been born in the State of Manhattan. This got a big laugh from the soldier and the gate guard, which really puzzled the boys. The soldier, who was a Jewish American, explained to the boys that Manhattan was not a state but a part of New York City, which was in the state of New York.

Werner Nathan

They told him their dream was to immigrate to America. They were seeking help to reach this dream. The soldier, Pfc. Werner Nathan, told them of how he had left Austria with his family, fleeing the Nazis six years earlier with his aging parents. The parents' business had been destroyed during the Kristallnacht pogrom, which prompted them to flee. He also told them that shortly after arriving in the States, his parents had died.

Hank and Fred told the soldier who they were and that they were also now orphans. The similarities of their stories and histories were eerie. After that, they saw each other often, and he gave much needed support and first-hand advice to the boys on how to immigrate. And he continued to offer help when needed.

Finally the Sun Breaks Through: Late 1945–1946

Chapter 16

In May, 1945, the US files a patent on the hydrogen bomb.

On August 6, 1945, the first atomic bomb is dropped on Hiroshima, Japan.

On August 9, the second atomic bomb is dropped on Nagasaki, Japan.

Japan announces its surrender to the Allies on August 14.

On September 2, 1945, Japan signs a formal surrender agreement aboard the USS Missouri in Tokyo Bay.

Tokyo Rose is arrested and sentenced to 10 years in prison.

In October, the United Nations is born.

The Nuremberg war crimes trials open.

Bikini swimwear is introduced to the world and causes a bigger stir than atomic tests on Bikini Atoll in the Marshall Islands.

A displaced person, by definition, is a person driven or expelled from his home or homeland by war or tyranny. The Jews of WWII certainly fit this bill. All over the world they had been driven, hounded, and hunted by the Nazis. As the Allied troops moved across Europe in 1944 and 1945, they came across displaced persons. They were taking shelter anywhere they could, while others struggled to stay alive in the monstrous death factories that had been left behind. The Allies were not prepared for what they found. In thousands of places they found these DPs and didn't know what to do with them. Many of those left behind were Jews, but there were many others, including some Allied soldiers of war, sympathizers, huge numbers of slave laborers of diverse nationalities, and those that Hitler just wanted to be rid of.

As the Allies liberated these people, they were overwhelmed by the poor conditions of those they found, as many if not most were near death and very frail. They had absolutely nothing, and they needed and were given medical care as well as food and water. In many instances, camps were simply abandoned by the Nazis as the Allies approached and the prisoners were left to starve. In Dachau, unguarded boxcars were found holding thousands of newly arrived prisoners, and out of 5,000, about 3,000 had already died before they could be released. Thousands more would die as a result of the conditions they were left in, during the days and weeks ahead. Individual and mass graves had to be dug across Europe, a chilling but sadly, not an uncommon task as the many dead and nearly dead were discovered.

The Allies now contemplated where to put these barely living people. For the time being, they were simply held in the camps where they had been found, sleeping in their bunks with only prison garb to wear. In many cases, they were held under armed guard. At least they were now getting food and water. Life tried to return to normal across the regions for most of the population, but not for the displaced persons. The Allies were afraid to just turn them loose. The DPs were just too weak to survive without some help; they also had no idea if their homes or families still existed and no means of trying to contact any relatives. There was also the worry about what these people would do to the civilian population once freed. They couldn't be just left to roam. Would revenge be on their minds or would blame be placed on them?

Most of these Jews wanted to go to Palestine, but the British who controlled the area would only allow 18,000 per year to emigrate there. This would continue to be the policy until 1947, when the British gave up control, and the state of Israel and a separate Arab state were established. In the meantime, President Truman of the United States established major changes in how the DPs would be treated, setting up camps for them throughout Europe, making the camps more humane, and loosening the immigration laws of the US. Thousands of DPs made their way to the States. President Truman placed orphans as a top priority.

People like Hank and Fred, although they truly were displaced, didn't follow the norm. They had survived underground and were therefore not found in a camp. They had to find other means of realizing their dream of living in America. They also had no identification of any kind or any known surviving relatives.

Since the time when Werner Nathan met the boys back at the gate to the US Army base, he had been helping the boys start the preparations for their eventual embarkation to America. This help turned out to be completely invaluable to them. He turned to his Lieutenant, Lt. Kowalski, who was also an American Jewish serviceman and who had, years before, immigrated to the United States from Europe. He jumped right in there and helped in many ways.

Most importantly, he got involved in the American Jewish Joint Distribution Committee (JDC), a Jewish assistance organization that employed many specialists on emigration procedures. The JDC quickly got the paperwork started that the newly created Central Committee of Liberated Jews in the American Occupied Zone (USCC) required, along with other necessary information.

It was found that the boys needed to come up with certain necessary documents to be able to apply for US visas. The two servicemen also recommended to Fred and Hank that they learn some English, any way that they could.

Three documents seemed to be needed, and the boys did not possess any of them. So they set out to find them. First, they set out to find both of their birth certificates. Since most offices were either closed or destroyed due to the just-ended war, this turned out not to be an easy task, but somehow the boys stumbled across the Office of Vital Statistics, which was operating as best it could, considering the situation. Most documents had been destroyed in the war.

Protocol was very lax and the manner in which their birth documents were prepared, strangely, was quite amusing. Paper was scarce, so the clerk used some slips that previously had been used by a worker during the war to make personal transfers to his bank account in Greece. Then the clerk stamped the papers and the boys were assured that these papers were official and that they would have no problem using them.

They then found out that the clerk could also help them get an official death certificate for their mother. First, they had to identify where they had last seen their mother alive and, if they could remember, what she was last seen wearing. Then the clerk began showing them pictures of women found dead in that vicinity on or around the date when they had last seen her. Both Hank and Fred quickly detached themselves from such grim views, not needing to be reminded of the tragic effects of war and of all the dead bodies they had seen during those last days of war.

The clerk asked them if any of the pictures had a corpse that was wearing clothes similar to what their mother had been wearing. The boys finally pointed to one, really just to end the ordeal. Next, the clerk took out a divorce document, filled in a few blanks, then crossed out "divorce" and inserted "death." Thus the process was completed with a stamp, certifying their mother's demise. Although quick, it was an awful experience, and definitely one the boys would never wish on someone else.

Then, with Pfc. Nathan' help, they filled out the visa information requests and filed them with the American visa office. It was early February and Nathan, along with Lt. Kowalski, had a very special surprise for Hank and Fred. The men had been busy planning a bar mitzvah for each of the boys, an event that all Jewish boys normally anticipate but one that had been completely forgotten in the midst of war and the loss of family members. Nathan and Kowalski had basically adopted the boys, and both being Orthodox Jews, they knew how important it was that the faith's traditions continue. They personally took to preparing them for the necessary Hebrew recitations of portions of the Torah and essential prayers.

The Old Synagogue, which the Tauchers had attended before it was shut down in 1938, was one of the first to reopen in Berlin after the war. Hank, Fred, Nathan, and Lt. Kowalski attended the Jewish New Year services there in September of 1945. The synagogue had for many years been used to store loot confiscated by the Germans, mostly from Jewish households, before being heavily damaged in the bombings of Berlin. Only one wing survived, which could hold about 200 worshipers. Later, Hank and Fred would have their bar mitzvahs there, on February 2, 1946. Fred had just turned 13, the age at which most Jewish males undergo this ritual, and he and Hank believe they were probably the first to celebrate their bar mitzvahs in Berlin after the war.

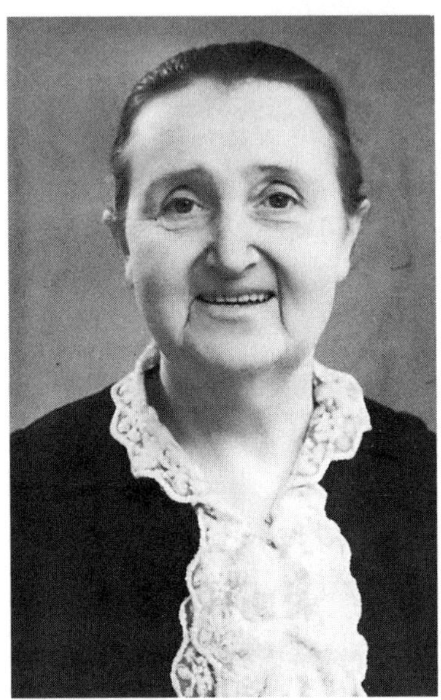

Gertrude Nölting

Traute Holina and the boys.

While waiting for their visas, Hank and Fred also attended the newly reopened German public schools, trying to stay up on their studies so they could fit in with similarly aged students upon reaching America. In early August, the boys told Gertrude and Traute that they had applied for their visas to go to America and might receive them very shortly. Gertrude's first words were "Boys, you can't go to America. Americans are our ENEMIES!" She was still in a strange denial that Germany had actually lost the war. She had removed anything and everything that had a Hitler or Nazi connection from her house, to avoid being linked to him.

Hank and Fred greeted the gentile New Year of 1946 while still living with Gertrude, ever careful not to show their aspirations of resettling in America at the earliest possible chance. They did not broach this subject with her, as they knew her hope was for the boys to stay on with her indefinitely, making their own lives in Germany. The mere mention of America would so anger her that the boys avoided the subject with her altogether.

Gertrude did sign both boys up for English lessons, taught by a German teacher who had never been outside of Germany and had learned his English strictly from friends, during college. After just a week or two of giving the boys English lessons, the teacher informed Fred that he had better not go to America and told him, "You just do not have the talent to learn English ever and so you better remain in Germany." This of course made Fred feel horrible, and he began to have second thoughts about going to America. But he remained determined that he would go, regardless of whether he might never be able to learn English.

In July, the JDC sent the boys about three hours from Berlin, to Lüneburg Children's Orphanage and School. At the time, sending parentless children to orphanages was a common practice among relief organizations across Europe and was intended to ensure that the children were in good medical and mental states. An orphanage was also a good place for the children to learn English and just relax for a time, while around other kids of similar ages. For many this was their first formal schooling.

On August 23, 1946, the Office of the Magistrate of Berlin issued Fred a document acknowledging that because he had been arrested and shipped off to a camp Fred had been a victim of fascism. This document allowed Fred and Hank free movement around Berlin and allowed them to get priority positions at soup kitchens and other places of relief services.

Group portrait of students and teachers at Lüneburg. Fred is among the group, as is Dorothea Isaacsohn. Her father was the first victim of the infamous Catchers, Stella and Rolf. Rolf was Dorothea's father's cousin. Dorothea survived by living underground with her mother in Germany and Poland.

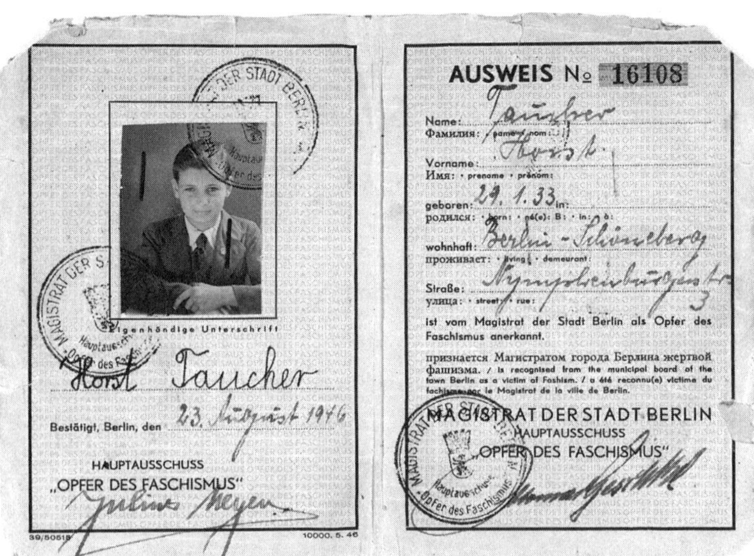

Fred's document from the Magistrate of Berlin.

Finally, in late August 1946, the boys' visas to the United States were approved, and they took an ambulance type Jeep with a member of the British Army as the driver to catch a US military transport plane when space became available. Upon arrival at the airfield, they were told that there was no space available on that flight but that they could board a ship at the nearby port. The next day, all arrangements were finalized, and the boys boarded a ship at Bremer Hafen on September 6, 1946. The fare of $135.00 each was paid by the Joint Distribution Committee (JDC) to the USCC, which in turn paid the shipping company.

Once on the ship, Hank was seasick for part of the 10-day voyage, which was very common on the long Atlantic crossing as winter approached. He finally got his sea legs a few days out. Many passengers had never even seen an ocean before, and on many of the ships seasickness seemed overly common. Many in this period of Atlantic crossings commented that it seemed as though Mother Nature was upset and was making the sea especially rough due to the war.

Fred enjoyed exploring the ship and looking out over the waves, anticipating his first glimpse of America. While not doing this, he would use his very limited English to help fellow passengers get things at the ship's store, which was operated by only English-speaking clerks. Most passengers were German-, Polish-, and Yiddish-speaking, and Fred's limited English was better than none. He would stand in the line for them, sometimes earning a tip and sometimes not. Many customers wanted chewing gum but instead got shaving cream, due to Fred's limited pronunciation.

At last, New York. After 10 days at sea, there it was: the New York skyline. "Wow." They had made it. Facing New York City, the reality swiftly set in. "We're here, now what do we do?"

Chapter 17

*The S.S. Marine Marlin, a troop carrier built in Vancouver, Washington, USA,
is converted to a passenger carrier after the war.*

In 1892, Ellis Island had opened as an immigration station.

In 1897, a fire destroyed the station, and all records were lost.

*In 1900, the station reopened, with one strict restriction:
all construction must be fireproof.*

*Ellis Island closed in 1954 and was reopened on a
limited viewing basis from 1976–1984.*

*The Statue of Liberty was given to the people of America by the people of France
for the friendship the two countries developed during the American Revolution.*

*The 151-foot-tall statue stands on a 154-foot-tall base
and was dedicated in 1886.*

*In 1947, the New York Yankees win the World Series,
led by Joe DiMaggio and Lou Gehrig.*

*In 1947, the population of Missouri is 3.6 million, and it is ranked
37th out of 50 American states in income.*

*Missouri's official state motto is "The Show Me" state,
and its state animal is the mule.*

In 1914, the American Jewish Joint Distribution Committee
(JDC) was established in New York City. The JDC is non-
political and goes beyond the Jewish community. It is the largest
channel of aid from the Jewish community in North America,
providing help to hundreds of thousands in the Soviet Union
and Europe, as well as to smaller communities in Latin America,
Asia, and Africa. It is also very active in Israel. It does concentrate
on Jewish plights, but is always willing to respond anywhere that

humanitarian aid is needed, whether it's due to a tidal wave, hurricane, or man-made genocide.

After WWI, the JDC helped millions of Jews to avoid death by supplying them with medicine, food, and shelter. Before WWII, as well as during the war, its work helped over 120,000 Jews to escape from Germany and many others areas after they came under Nazi control. Right after the war, the JDC's first step was to get emergency supplies to the starving and homeless masses in Europe. There was much work to do before it could turn to helping additional thousands of Jews to escape war-torn Europe to either the US or to Israel. Also, millions more of the European Jews just wanted to return to their homes in Europe, which they had been forced to leave. Many were considered Displaced Persons. The JDC helped Israel to get established as an independent state. By the year 2000 it had helped millions and continues

A crowd celebrating the founding of the State of Israel, outside the headquarters of the Central Committee of the Liberated Jews, on May1, 1948, in Germany.

its traditions today, focusing on the Jewish plight but never turning its back on others' needs.

"Hey, Hank, this isn't Germany no more!" Fred and Hank were both standing near the bow of the *S.S. Marine Marlin* so that they could view both sides of the shoreline of their new country while a ship's crew member pointed out the sights to them and others that had gathered. After motoring for about an hour the ship was in the Upper Bay, with New York City and Governor Island on the right. To the left was the Jersey shoreline and Ellis Island, with the Statue of Liberty towering above it, directly behind. Hank and Fred knew that Ellis Island was where their visa and entry papers would be processed; from there, they had been told, they would be ferried over to New York City's waterfront and offloaded.

All kinds of thoughts were entering the boys' heads as the situation suddenly turned from a dream hatched in far-off, war-decimated Germany to the reality of a huge, bustling, cosmopolitan city. They had little money, mostly just coins; nowhere to stay; and no known relatives in America. Might they have any relative living in America, who might have escaped to America early on in Hitler's rule, who they did not know about? The boys decided that once processed, they would explore New York a bit, find a place to stay, and start the hunt for their new life in this strange land that would soon be their new home. They had forgotten in the excitement that a JDC representative was going to be at the Port to greet them when they disembarked the ship.

After standing awhile in line, they finally received a seat at an immigration desk. The immigration officials at the Port took pride in the fact that during this time it was the main port of entry into the US for immigrants arriving from all over Europe and that most immigrants were processed in about two hours. Once the clerk received the visas from Fred and Hank, she waved another lady over who introduced herself and said that she was from the Joint Distribution Committee and had been sent to help them. The boys were very relieved.

She proceeded with helping them get processed and then took them to a temporary orphanage that the JDC operated at 441 Caldwell, Bronx, NY. They now had completed their immigration to America and were finally official immigrants. Once at the orphanage they were interviewed by staff, and finally someone asked if they knew any relatives living in the United States. They could only answer that they did not know for sure but thought they might have two cousins who were brothers, somewhere in America, but they had no idea of their exact location.

The JDC began the search for the relatives using a tried-and-true method. An ad was placed in a worldwide newspaper printed in German, *Der Aufbau*, which served as a prime networking tool for survivors who were now living in the States and elsewhere, enabling many to find lost relatives. It turned out that there were two men who lived in Joplin, Missouri, who did not subscribe to the paper but had friends who did. Their friends asked them if they might have relatives from the old country looking for them. The men then called the JDC and were told that a Fred and Hank Taucher from Germany were looking for any relatives in America and that those relatives might be named Felix and Alfred Taucher.

Felix and Alfred Taucher were now wondering if indeed they had been found by some lost relatives, and it was quickly confirmed to the boys that the two men were indeed their cousins. Excitement was shared by all, the cousins hardly believing that somehow the boys had survived the Holocaust and were now in America. What about the rest of their relatives, did any others survive? The cousins could hardly wait to hear the rest of the story. The men told the JDC that they would be happy to accept Hank and Fred, along with the task of parenting.

This turned out to be just too easy, ah, as nothing is ever simple. Their offer was rejected because the cousins were both single, even though they both earned good incomes, one as a shirt factory worker and the other as a piano teacher and sales manager in one of the bigger department stores in Joplin, MO. They even supplemented their incomes with income from some rental properties that they owned. They owned and lived in an above-average house, in a Midwestern, blue collar town, but they lacked one major factor that they needed to host the boys as their foster parents. The single fact that there was no adult woman living in the household disqualified their application.

Swallowing this bitter news, the boys found themselves being placed in a foster home in Kansas City, Missouri, the residence of an Orthodox Jewish rabbi, his wife, and their two children. Hank and Fred were happy to be under a friendly roof, although deep down preferring to be with real family members. The boys then went to be enrolled in fall classes, and both were placed in their relative peer group, which was determined to be the eighth grade for both. Fred and Hank's mother, Therese, had done her best in getting the boys into schools in Germany before Hitler's ban on Jews' going to school took effect. She always also had spent as much time as possible homeschooling them. The war's outbreak really curtailed this, but the boys were smart and had seized every opportunity presented to learn, and they appeared ready for the new challenges.

Fall arrived and into school they went, with things going fairly well. Alfred, the cousin, would take the Greyhound bus north to see the boys every other weekend. He could see that the one problem that the boys were having was adjusting to life in such an extremely Orthodox household setting. The relief organization was asked for a change of houses for the boys. This was quickly granted, as an acceptable and receptive family happened to live nearby. Thus their schooling was not disrupted.

Meanwhile, Hank and Fred's uncles were working on getting the boys with them. A plan was hatched. They had a found an aunt living in Israel who wanted to move to the States. Eventually, Felix and Alfred agreed to sponsor her immigration, and she applied for her visa, which was soon granted. All went well, with the relative making an excellent "lady of the household," and the agency quickly granted the boys' move to their cousins' house in Joplin, Missouri. Everyone was waiting for the end of the school year in a few weeks, eagerly anticipating the big move.

Finally, the day came, and Felix drove the four hours down to Kansas City to collect the boys. All of them were bursting with the pent-up excitement of finally being united as a family. Tante, the aunt, was a wonderful choice to be the woman of the household, taking great care of all. Felix and Alfred did an excellent job of providing a nice home, complete with a family to be a part of.

The boys entered Joplin High School as sophomores and, although intimidated, they both did well in school. Fred especially did well in science and English. Early on, Fred would start up conversations with anyone, practicing so that he could speak like a native Midwesterner. Hank set about fitting in and found a love for the piano, learning from his cousin Alfred. The school years flew by, and after graduation both boys got entry-level positions at the department store where Alfred was a sales manager.

Life in America: Late 1950 and Beyond

Chapter 18

The ROTC program was very popular in the 1950–60s throughout the US. The Korean War effort needed well-trained officers and quickly. Many young ROTC high school and college youths were joining the war cause and were quickly made squad leaders and officers. The Korean conflict was never called a war in the US, as the US Congress never passed a declaration of war against North Korea. In 1950, North Korea invaded South Korea in what was a civil war. The North Korean troops quickly pushed their way through the South to the southern end of the Korean Peninsula. The United Nations then voted to send NATO troops to help the Democratic South, with the US Armed Forces providing the bulk of the support.

China and the USSR chose to support the Communist North. The South's forces quickly took back all of their losses and fought their way to the North's northern border with China.

Then, due to the huge support the North got from China, the fight continued, with things going the other way before finally stalling out near the original border between North and South Korea, the 38th parallel. Peace talks started in 1951 and finally, after two more years of bitter fighting, the North signed an armistice, which the South refused to participate in; thus, no peace treaty was ever completed and still has not been as 2010 comes to a close.

This, many believe, was the official beginning of the long-running cold war between the world's two superpowers: the USSR and the USA. America stood resolute in its fight against communism and its desire to see that capitalism and democracy stayed alive and well. In the Korean conflict, 33,500 US troops were killed, while 900,000 Chinese were killed. Over 2 million civilian lives were also lost.

Fred and Hank had both chosen to sign up, and they joined the Junior ROTC program, which was an optional activity for high school students. At the time, the JROTC program had a drill team, the Eveready Rifle Team, which they joined, performing during high school sports events and public parades. Both also applied for and began studying for their US citizenship test. Hank was the first to receive notice of where and when to take the test. Hank easily passed and received his citizenship in early 1952.

Fred, meanwhile, had applied to the Southeast Missouri State University and took the entrance exam. He kept this quiet, as he did not want anyone to know in case he failed the exam. Fred did get denied, because he had done too well on the English part of the exam. The faculty surmised that anyone whose education had been interrupted so many times and who did not have English as his native language could not post such high scores without having cheated. Appalled by this false judgment, Fred denied any wrongdoing and was still refused a chance to take a second exam.

The Korean conflict was urgently calling Americans into allied support, and although not yet a citizen of the United States, Fred was of draft age and wanted to do the right thing by his new country. After all, the US had helped to save him and his brother. A few months after graduation, he went down to a recruitment office along with four friends. They had all performed together in the Eveready drill team from JROTC, and they had all decided to join up. One chose the Air Force, while Fred and two others chose the US Army.

The three of them were quickly assigned to Fort Leonardwood, MO, for basic training. While there, they practiced the routines they had learned as members of their high school drill team, which really impressed their first sergeant and company commander, who appointed them to be squad leaders in their respective squadrons.

Hank was drafted into the US Army.

Putting aside his ambitions to be a pianist, Hank followed the instructions that he had received from the US Army and reported to Camp Breckenridge in Kentucky to begin basic training. Hank also quickly became a squad leader in his unit, due to his previous JROTC training.

After a short time, an opening came up for a company clerk position, which he applied for. It turned out he was well qualified for it, as he was very proficient in English, having received above average scores in high school, and his piano studies had instilled in him quick fingers. He could fly across the letters on a typewriter.

Following basic training, Fred was assigned to the 506th Replacement Company at Fort Leonard Wood, Missouri. After attending clerk typist school, Fred was given an assignment as a morning report clerk and then became a corporal shortly thereafter, a rank he held until June, 1952. He was most pleased when told that he would have the opportunity to take his citizenship examination, naturally assuming he could not take part in any military operations until he was naturalized. He then took the exam and waited confidently for the results. He was told by those in charge not to worry, his official documentation would reach his overseas post.

That month he received orders to go to Germany. Apparently, a general was requesting a chauffeur who spoke the native language. Obviously, the officer who was handling this request believed Fred to be an excellent candidate, but no matter how much the officer may have insisted on this, Fred would not agree to this directive. The officer was seemingly unsympathetic to the forcibly intense suffering and loss which Fred had experienced growing up and was unable to appreciate how deeply Fred then wanted nothing to do with returning to Germany and speaking that language. Fred had to turn to his personnel officer, who in turn enlisted his inspector general to look into Fred's request for an assignment change.

Fred's reluctance must have not put him in good stead, as he was promptly deployed to Asia, by way of Fort Lewis in the state of Washington. During his 10 days at Ft. Lewis, he visited Seattle, which was only a one and a half hour bus ride from the base, every chance he had. Upon becoming familiar with the area, he fell in love with it. At the time, he said to himself, "If I make it back alive from Korea, I will settle down in Washington State."

In Korea, he was appointed as a warrant officer with the 25th Infantry Division. Fred's new duty in Korea was picking up field casualty reports from various companies from the 25th Infantry Division and auditing them before the information was entered on to IBM machines with punched cards for later delivery to the 96th Machine Records Unit in Tokyo. It was a responsibility Fred held with noble honor.

Fred became the fifth officer to hold this job in his unit in a short period of time, due to others going missing or being killed. It seemed like a job no one wanted, but Fred knew it was necessary and important. His work area was inside of two 18-wheel tractor-trailer rigs. One rig was used as the office and the other held power-supplying equipment and data processing machines. The most dangerous parts of the job were the treks out to the front line command posts to pick up casualties reports and the return trips. Fred would always be accompanied by a Korean officer whose job was to supply sniper protection as well to scout for mines on the paths.

When the conflict in Korea came to an end in July, 1953, he was reassigned to Tokyo, where he resumed his administrative office work, eventually landing at the large barracks of Camp Zama, near the Atsugi Naval Airbase in Japan. Fred also attended a number of training classes to heighten his expertise in data processing and machine accounting equipment. He also learned the Japanese language while stationed there.

Early in 1953, his unit in Camp Zama took delivery of the newest data processing equipment, which was a great improvement from the WWII punch card equipment he had used in Korea and also in Japan when he was first stationed there. This new equipment still relied on punch cards, but was much faster than what he had had access to prior to that time and could handle a lot more information. This upgrade resulted in his having a small amount of free time. In the evenings he took up studying martial arts at the Kodokan Judo Institute in Tokyo.

Upon his return stateside in May, 1954, Fred was sent to Ft. Carson, where preparations would be made for his discharge. He believed that this would be a relatively simple process, but a circus of errors was revealed, stemming from the issue of citizenship. In essence, Fred should not have been serving any time in Korea as an officer since it was mandatory that only someone with a minimum of 10 years' citizenship be situated with the assignment he held there.

The army was aware of his having taken the exam back in Rolla, Missouri, some years earlier, but the records, which he had been informed would follow him to Korea, were mistakenly sent to Germany and completely lost. After jumping through hoops for military and legal authorities, the coup de grace was that "he would not receive an honorable discharge from his rank of Warrant Officer, but would have to accept the lower, noncommissioned status of Sergeant E-5."

Fred really wanted to re-enlist after only a few days of R&R, but the prospect of not retaining his warrant officer rating should he re-enlist finally made up his mind for him. He just accepted his honorable discharge as a sergeant, thus ending his service duties. His longer term, serious intention was actually to shine in a business of his own making, in the footsteps of his father, so that one day he would have no need to endure the orders of others.

An additional caveat was that he could not admit to his actual duty in the Korean conflict for 10 years. As for the nagging issue of his citizenship, prior to his discharge the army arranged a special hearing for him to be sworn in as a United States citizen back in Rolla, Missouri, where he had initially taken his examination for citizenship. After the swearing-in ceremony, the judge congratulated him for becoming a US citizen and also made it a point to thank him for his military service in the US Armed Forces. "Wow, I am finally a full-fledged American citizen."

There were numerous pluses in Fred's military experience, most significant the advantage of a hands-on education in the usage and components of business automation systems. Once back in civilian clothes, he returned to Joplin, Missouri, and stayed with Felix and Alfred for maybe six weeks, contemplating his vista of the brand new world of office automation. In those days, computers were not yet being used in small and medium-sized private businesses.

He felt quite stressed following his army service and needed time to regroup and see if he could find some work, but despite his attempts, at that point very few businesses in Joplin had implemented the IBM equipment on which he had been trained. It was now getting toward the end of June, the weather was extremely hot, and his concerns about finding any prospects of work in Joplin were only adding to Fred's discomfort. Fred decided to adopt the old adage "Go west, young man." He had seen an ad for a person to drive a car to the West Coast for a dealership, so he packed up what little he had, took the job, and drove out to the Pacific Northwest to find a new life and career.

Hank, meanwhile, was finishing his first stint in the military and would be discharged on August 18, 1954, as a corporal. With the Korean conflict over, he also found the civilian job market extremely tight, with wages low. Hank decided that the army's offer to let anyone who had been discharged re-enter at his or her previous rank, if they did so within 89 days, was his best choice. So he re-enlisted and was sent to Fort Hood, Texas, in November, 1954. At that point, he decided to make the US Army his life and career.

Hank had a highly successful career in the army, and his duties took him around the world. His career followed the traditional climb up the ladder of rank, from corporal to sergeant, warrant officer, first lieutenant, captain, and, finally, major. He experienced many duties and tours, including active leadership under enemy fire in Vietnam. He finally landed in England, where he worked within the State Department of Defense, handling administrative requirements in assistance to various Allied commanders. He retired as a major in January of 1974. Hank would always take any opportunity to play the piano, either for small or large groups, wherever he was, and he still does enjoy playing. He is currently living in Southern California with his wife of 45 years and their pets.

MAJOR
HENRY (HANK) E. TAUCHER,
US ARMY RETIRED

Decorations and Awards
- Good Conduct Medal (3 Loops)
- National Defense Service Medal (Oak Leaf Cluster)
- Army Commendation Medal (Oak Leaf Cluster)
- Vietnam Service Medal
- Vietnam Campaign Medal
- Armed Forces Reserve Medal
- Bronze Star Legion of Merit: Presidential
- Unit Citation: Meritorious
- Unit Commendation: Gallantry Cross with Palm
- Letters of Commendation
- Certificates of Achievement

FRED H. TAUCHER

- President & CEO of Corporate Management Inc.
- Chairman & CEO of Corporate Computer Inc.
- First Lieutenant, US Civil Air Patrol
- Holocaust Survivor Foundation USA, serving on the Executive Committee (HSF-USA)
- Member, Washington State Holocaust Education Resource Center, Speakers Bureau
- Life Member, Military Officers Association of America (MOAA)
- Member, American Legion
- Life Member, Veterans of Foreign Wars (VFW)
- Life Member, Disabled American Veterans (DAV)
- Life Member, Everett Navy League
- Washington State Olympic Committee
- Member, English Speaking Union
- Seattle-Kobe Sister Cities Association, Past President
- Japan America Society of Washington State, Past Board of Directors
- Washington State China Relations Council
- Trade Development Alliance of Seattle, Advisory Board

Epilogue:
Four Full Seasons

The Civil Air Patrol is created in 1941 to assist in the war effort.

*The end of WWII brings about the baby boom in the US,
with 77.3 million born from 1946 to 1964.*

In 1954, the Boeing 707, the first commercial jet transport, is introduced.

*In 1955, Rosa Parks, an African-American, refuses to give up her seat
on a bus to a white person.*

In 1962, the Seattle World's Fair opens with a futuristic science theme.

In 1964, guitarist Jimmy Hendrix, a Seattle native, dies from a drug overdose.

*In 1964, civil rights legislation passed in the US bans discrimination
based on race, color, religion, and gender.*

In 1974, Microsoft goes public.

In 1989, the Berlin Wall comes down.

*In 1994, 1 million Rwandans are killed in 100 days in ethnic fighting.
The Hutus want to eliminate the Tutsis.*

In 1995, an agreement is signed ending genocide in Srebrenica.

*In January 2010, the Rwanda holocaust continues, having spilled into
the DR Congo. The death toll stands at approximately 5 million,
with rape being used as a tool of war.*

In 2010, France begins targeting illegal Roma immigrants for deportation.

Washington State is the contiguous US's most northwestern state, with Vancouver, Canada its neighbor to the north. Seattle lies on Puget Sound, which leads out to the Pacific Ocean. Having numerous harbors makes it an ideal place for maritime trade serving Alaska, Canada, and other Pacific Rim ports, such as Hong Kong and Kobe, Japan. Two mountain ranges and numerous snow-covered volcanoes dot the views. Lakes, sounds, rivers, rain forests, deserts, and island chains make for numerous places to enjoy outdoor activities year round. Cultural events and the arts are also numerous.

A town of numerous booms and busts, Seattle first had a booming lumber industry, followed by a boom during the Alaska Gold Rush era. A few years later, business was booming again as workers in Seattle were busy building ships for WWI, then airplanes for WWII, and then passenger planes. After WWII, with the military not buying many planes, Seattle suffered a major bust as Boeing factories sat empty and 70,000 workers were laid off. But this was short-lived, as after the war Americans took to traveling by commercial jet aircraft in huge numbers. Freeways and bridges were also being built to get all the workers to their jobs from the surrounding neighborhoods. Then along came the 1964 World's Fair. The Fair was a rousing success, revitalizing the decaying downtown area and leaving behind stadiums, cultural art centers, the Pacific Science Center, and the famous Space Needle. The Pike Place market, as well as Pioneer Square, also found new (boom) life after the earlier Boeing bust.

Fred had recalled Washington State as an extremely likable place that was attractive not only because of its temperate and seasonal climate. Fred decided to move there in the early 1950s, and settled first in the city of Seattle and later in Edmonds, just a few minutes' drive north of Seattle. The other reason, besides the climate, that he chose the area was his knowledge of the state's being ahead of the curve in advanced technologies, with its economy supported by prodigious corporations, of which Boeing was just one of many making Washington their home base.

Shortly after his military service ended, an event changed Fred's life forever. During a visit to New York, Fred took time to revisit some of the places Hank and he had first come to know following their journey to America in 1946, such as the orphan home where they had first lived. Fred got off at the Bronx subway station nearest to Caldwell Avenue, but found that the orphan home's old address now belonged to another party and that no one around had any recollection of the home that had been there in previous years. As Fred walked around the neighborhood a bit, he caught sight of an older lady who appeared destitute and frail. It made him sad to see her, and as Fred moved closer he saw, to his heartbreak, that she wore the number tattoo on her arm.

Fred asked if the numbers represented her being imprisoned at Auschwitz, knowing full well that this was the case. Not knowing English well, she reluctantly confirmed in Yiddish the same, saying she was a survivor, living on very little subsidy, with barely enough to pay for medicine and with a three-day wait before getting help from the JDC for food and her other bare essentials.

When Fred asked her age she hesitated, then admitted to being 87 years old and the sole survivor of her entire family. "She could have been my mother." Again Fred pressed her to take a little money, but she was shaking her head as if to say "I am neither poor nor desperate." She turned and disappeared around the corner. Fred made up his mind right there that, as soon as he possibly could, he would get involved in holocaust survivorship assistance and service.

The fact is, the world was entering the computer age, and Fred wanted in on the action. Much progress would be made on his business front, with him continually staying up-to-date on many of the developments in the computer industry, especially those having to do with data management. Processing speed and the complexities of data masses were growing at rapidly exponential compounding rates. Businesses needed software and hardware managers to handle their new sophisticated needs.

In 1979, Bill Gates and Paul Allen brought Microsoft, the company that they had founded in New Mexico, to their home area in Redmond, Washington. In1985, sales were around $150 million, in 1990 sales hit the billion dollar mark, and in 1999 Microsoft would become the world's most profitable company. Suddenly, there were millionaires everywhere, with many starting up their own companies.

After many years working for others or as a part-owner, a truly fulfilling result of Fred's career growth occurred. He had become associated with the Seattle-based company Corporate Management Inc. in 1963. He then became president and majority stockholder in 1968. He also established, in 1985, a separate company, Corporate Computer Inc., to handle other solutions for different clients, with newly emerging products and services in the field of computers.

Over the years, both companies have thrived, evolving and keeping pace with the technological progress of the industry. CCI was one of the first 10 Microsoft Solution Partners. Another highlight for Fred was the company's being chosen to do custom software for the European Space Administration in Darmstadt, Germany.

This entailed yearly visits to the facility for several years. Sadly, Microsoft ceased support of this custom operating software that was required by the European Space Administration.

Presently, CCI and CMI focus on supporting wide area networks and computer systems, mainly for law firms and for companies that network several hundred computers at any given time. This service also includes solving computer problems remotely from the Seattle-based office to any destination in the world, as long as the client can get on the Internet.

Seattle also hosted a meeting of the World Trade Organization in 1999, at which time a very large confrontation occurred in which the anti-corporate globalization folks rioted for three days and nights. Fred was there as a volunteer doing translation work for some of the different attendees, as he speaks German, Japanese, and English. He often had to sneak through the crowds to get to the meetings, incognito. He said it was like WWII all over again.

Fred enjoys piloting small aircraft and has earned his private FAA certified pilots license. Once he was qualified, he joined the Civil Air Patrol (CAP). He found that it offered a rewarding opportunity to use his own small plane in important causes, which was far better than just using his plane solely for personal and business purposes.

The CAP was used in WWII for patrols of American shorelines to watch for enemy submarines, as well as to help look for downed military aircraft during training exercises in the States. During the war, CAP sighted 173 enemy submarines and actually sank two. It is a volunteer organization of aviation-minded civilians.

Although known primarily for its search and rescue operations, as well as for its emergency flights, in recent years it has seen its border patrol missions increase, as well as its role in assisting drug patrols. CAP's flights were the first allowed into the World Trade Tower airspace to survey and photograph the damage after the 9/11 attacks, at a time when all other flights, both commercial as well as private, were grounded throughout the entire US. Fred proudly now has a grandson in the program.

In acknowledging the urge to find public forums in which to speak out about the Holocaust and to meet with fellow survivors, it should come as no surprise that baring his soul in public settings has not been easy for him, though as with most things, his comfort level improves each time he speaks. In one of the first newspaper articles written about him, he shared his feelings, which for many, many years had been kept bottled up. He did not want to talk about his horrendous experiences. He had a hard time believing the terrible things that had happened to him just because he was born Jewish in the wrong country at the wrong time. These are stories that should be told and not be forgotten, he keeps reminding himself.

When Fred decided he wanted to speak boldly about what Hank and he had experienced, he was not so much motivated by personal satisfaction as by a profound desire to educate others about the history of the Holocaust. He saw a means by which others would become enlightened as to how negative perceptions and ignorance bred through the ages had served no one, especially not the Jewish people against whom this hatred was promoted. With educational institutions being the obvious venue, Fred has received very welcome offers from many high schools and colleges, civic groups, synagogues, and churches. Fred has also spoken at Holocaust museums and memorials in Berlin, Germany, and the Holocaust Education Center in Tokyo, Japan, as well as similar institutes here in America.

Every year, Fred is usually invited to speak at military installations in Washington State during Holocaust Remembrance Week (Yom Hashoah). He finds these occasions especially moving as in many instances the personnel are getting ready to deploy to war zones in the near future in various parts of the world, with little idea of what lies ahead for them. One time he gave a talk to the crew of the USS *Abraham Lincoln* a Nimitz-class type aircraft carrier. Having the chance to see and talk to an actual survivor of genocide and ethnic cleansing helped give the sailors a better understanding of why they were being called to fight.

Fred talks at a high school classroom in Edmonds, WA, about his experiences as a young Jewish boy.

Hank and Fred would keep in touch throughout the years, sometimes living only a few miles apart and at other times miles and countries apart. One common subject that they spoke about was about the many good German people who had helped the family during the Holocaust. As they grew older and understood the times better, they realized that the number of times help was offered to them was truly amazing. The tremendous risk at which these people had placed themselves and the ones they loved was mindboggling. The list was a long one and seemed to grow as the years went by.

Remember the little girl in the subway shelter? She would tell the boys years later that she had figured out at that time that they were not really shy but must have been Jewish, and she had just kept it to herself. Another young girl had hidden behind her closed curtains and watched the family visit Gertrude and Traute's home, which was next door, and she had also suspected they were Jewish. The young girl was puzzled by the fact that Traute, who wore an SS uniform, would have Jewish visitors, but she too had kept quiet, never bothering to tell her parents. Fred and Hank would never know the exact number of good Germans who had helped them, through small and large deeds, but it was indeed large enough to allow them to forgive most German people.

This woman, now elderly, told Fred that the two women that he and his brother had stayed with were not mother and daughter. She said they were a gay couple who had kept their relationship hidden so that the Nazis wouldn't find out about it. Fred has always wondered why the ladies helped them out so much; he doubts if this explanation is actually true and, in any case, it is completely irrelevant. He feels the help was given when the enormous evils that Hitler had sown erupted against so many actual individuals, at which point people realized that Hitler and his followers had simply gone just too far.

Recently, Fred went to Prague for a World Conference of Jewish Children who survived the Holocaust, and he was reunited with one of the children from the Lüneburg Children's Orphanage and School in Germany. She was stunned when she was introduced to Fred, as she and all the other children at the school believed that both he and Henry had died in a plane crash. It turned out that the plane the boys should have flown on when they left Germany in 1946 had disappeared over the Atlantic, and all were presumed dead. The kids at the school had felt so sad that two of their group had come so close to beginning a new life, only to have it snatched away.

"Hope springs eternal" is a saying Fred tries to live by. He has been lifted out of the quicksand of impending death and then seen the way toward groundbreaking frontiers. He still is busy in the business world and in many different business and civic organizations and is always willing to share knowledge he has gained in his long business career and through his life experiences. His sharing of his family's story is a small effort to contribute toward working to make the world a better place for all.

About the Author

Craig A. Ledbetter lives in Costa Rica, where he continues to pursue his passion for fishing in the rich Big Game waters of the Pacific Ocean off the Central American coastline. He has 30 years of experience as a sport fishing Captain and owner/operator. His home is near the beach in the northwest of Costa Rica, by the small town of Playa Potrero. He has written numerous magazine and newspaper articles, in both English and Spanish. He graduated from The Overlake High School in Redmond, WA, and then majored in Business/Economics at Eastern Oregon State University. His black Labrador is named Spot.